MEASURING THE PERFORMANCE OF INTERLIBRARY LOAN OPERATIONS IN NORTH AMERICAN RESEARCH AND COLLEGE LIBRARIES

Results of a study funded by
The Andrew W. Mellon Foundation

by

Mary E. Jackson
ARL Access & Delivery Services Consultant

Association of Research Libraries
Washington, DC
1998

MEASURING THE PERFORMANCE OF INTERLIBRARY LOAN OPERATIONS IN NORTH AMERICAN RESEARCH AND COLLEGE LIBRARIES

Results of a study funded by
The Andrew W. Mellon Foundation

Mary E. Jackson

Association of Research Libraries
21 Dupont Circle, N.W., Suite 800
Washington, DC 20036-1118
202-296-2296 (phone)
202-872-0884 (fax)
pubs@arl.org

ISBN: 0-918006-33-3

TABLE OF CONTENTS

1 Introduction

2 Follow-up Examination of Research Libraries with High and Low Unit Cost ILL Operations

3 Performance of ILL/DD Operations in 119 Research and College Libraries in 1996

8 Conclusions

Appendices

TABLES

FIGURES

FOREWORD

The findings of the ARL ILL/DD Performance Measures Study presented here were made possible by a major grant from The Andrew W. Mellon Foundation; contributions by staff in the 119 participating libraries; and strong support from Duane Webster, Executive Director, and other key staff of the Association of Research Libraries. The study builds on a record of scholarship on interlibrary loan performance and costs over several decades.

The ILL/DD Performance Measures Study is part of a multi-year effort led by the Association of Research Libraries, with the aim to increase access to library resources among libraries while reducing costs. In recent years resource sharing has grown in importance to libraries because libraries are no longer able to collect comprehensively and also because of steep increases in the volume and price of publications. Thus, libraries have invented new ways of sharing resources and are working to improve the still-useful old way, that is, interlibrary loan. Interlibrary loan has become a critical success factor for libraries of all types.

The increasing importance of interlibrary loan has led to this examination of its performance, processes, and costs. One might say that those of us working to improve interlibrary loan hoped to effect change as dramatic as that which occurred in cataloging with the advent of OCLC. Although important work has been done, we are not there yet.

This report outlines current interlibrary loan performance and cost measures. It exemplifies a great range of performance: from incredibly slow, expensive, and fallible, to amazingly fast, cheap, and reliable. By comparing the quantitative results in this report with those of the 1992 ARL/RLG Interlibrary Loan Cost Study, we see that ILL costs have come down, reversing a twenty-year trend. This report describes in detail both the changes in ILL costs and other measures of performance.

The purpose of this particular report is essentially descriptive, to characterize the research and its findings. It does not prescribe how change might be effected in an organization so one could emulate the amazingly fast, cheap, and reliable libraries. However, administrators can look at this report (and for the study participants, compare it to their own data) and ask useful questions. Why are the successful successful?

From listening to the libraries identified in this study as best performers, I have discerned four characteristics the successful have in common: They make intensive use of technology for every step in the process, and build that technology when it is not commercially available. They routinely question every step in their processes and regularly make improvements and adjustments (that is, they think about how they are working as they work). They value service more than control, and are willing to risk occasional errors for faster or better service. Finally, their library directors are intensely interested in and enthusiastic supporters of their efforts.

Although this report is not itself a change agent, its findings will be the basis for ARL-designed workshops intended to effect change. The ARL workshops will be structured to assist libraries in evaluating and adapting the findings of the study to their own libraries. In addition, ARL is testing the viability of making institution-specific site visits to reengineer local interlibrary loan operations. The first such test is underway with Mary Jackson, ARL Access & Delivery Services Consultant, working with Washington University Libraries staff in a best practices team whose charge is to improve and replicate in our library the practices of one of the identified best practice sites, Colorado State University Libraries. This endeavor will touch not only Washington University but also our partners in the Missouri Research Consortium of Libraries (MIRACL), the University of Missouri–Columbia, University of Missouri–Kansas City, University of Missouri–Rolla, University of Missouri–St. Louis, and Saint Louis University. Our five partner institutions are assigning staff to work with Jackson and the Washington University team in order to carry the results of our findings to all six institutions.

The publication of *Measuring the Performance of Interlibrary Loan Operations in North American Research and College Libraries* signifies the completion of the analysis phase. The next step is action—action to make not incremental but astounding improvements in the performance of every library's interlibrary loan unit. We have learned from the best performers that even the best can get better, and the benefits accrue to us all.

Shirley K. Baker
Vice Chancellor for Information Technology and
    Dean of University Libraries
Washington University in St. Louis
St. Louis, Missouri
March 20, 1998

ACKNOWLEDGMENTS

This Study would not have been possible without the interest and support of a number of individuals. Dr. Martin M. Cummings, Council on Library and Information Resources Consultant, first approached ARL with the idea of exploring in greater detail the economics of interlibrary loan and document delivery; he also provided ongoing guidance and advice on the methodology for this Study. The Andrew W. Mellon Foundation provided financial support without which the Study would not have been possible. Richard W. Ekman, Secretary of The Andrew W. Mellon Foundation, oversaw the grant award and provided ongoing encouragement and advice. James Michalko, President of the Research Libraries Group, agreed to permit ARL to revise the cost instruments developed by RLG and used in the 1992 ARL/RLG ILL Cost Study.

A number of library directors served on the Study's Advisory Committee. Shirley Baker, Washington University in St. Louis, chaired the Committee. She was joined by William Crowe, University of Kansas; William Studer, Ohio State University; Kent Hendrickson, University of Nebraska; and Paul Kobulnicky, University of Connecticut. Each served as a liaison to an ARL Standing Committee. An additional member of the Study's Advisory Committee, Barbara Brown, Washington and Lee University, was instrumental in securing participation of the Oberlin Group libraries and served as liaison to the college library participants. All committee members commented on various drafts, reacted to preliminary findings, and reviewed the final report.

Dr. Michael McPherson, Williams College, served as consulting economist until his appointment as President of Macalester College in May 1996. Dr. Bruce Kingma, University at Albany, then assumed that role. Dr. Kingma also managed the input of the raw data. Appreciation is also extended to his assistant, Susan Funk, and the cadre of University at Albany students who keyed in data from over 14,000 forms: Tammie Alzona, Cathie Bashaw, Mary Ann Dean, Aimee Dean, Michelle Eichelberger, Michael Fillinger, Daniel Funk, Rebekah Funk, Helene Gold, Sarah Hinman, Susan Kingma, Naomi Lapo, Maureen Logan, Michelle Moorhead, Tsering Shawa, and Leticia Sotelo.

Other key individuals included Marilyn Roche, author of the *ARL/RLG Interlibrary Loan Cost Study*, who provided valuable historical context and critical review of the findings, and Kendon Stubbs, University of Virginia and Consultant to the ARL Statistics and Measurement Committee, who reviewed the findings as they relate to ARL's statistical capability. Larry Frye, Director of the Wabash College Library, supplied FY96 data for the Oberlin Group members.

Staff at OCLC and the Research Libraries Group provided unpublished data used in several sections of the report. These data were instrumental in placing the findings of this Study into a larger context.

Completing the group that reviewed and commented on the final draft were Sarah Pritchard, Director of the Smith College Library; Carolynne Presser, Director of the University of Manitoba Libraries; and Carrol Lunau, Resource Sharing Officer, National Library of Canada.

A number of ARL staff provided help and advice during the entire process. Jaia Barrett provided invaluable guidance, asked probing questions, and helped keep the project focused and on target. The ARL Publications staff assisted in the preparation of press releases and articles as well as production and editing of the final report. Martha Kyrillidou and Julia Blixrud shared their expertise with statistics and data collection. Mary Jane Brooks managed multiple mailings and receipt of user satisfaction surveys.

To the directors and ILL managers of the 119 participating libraries, a heartfelt thanks. Without the encouragement of senior administrators and the active involvement of ILL managers, this Study would not have been completed. Gathering a wealth of detailed statistical information and tracking many user satisfaction surveys while managing active ILL operations required a commitment to the Study reflective of the service-oriented philosophy of ILL managers. Finally, to the patrons in the participating institutions, a special thank you for completing the surveys and sharing your views about current ILL services.

Mary E. Jackson
Principal Investigator & ARL Access & Delivery
   Services Consultant
Association of Research Libraries
March 1998

MEASURING THE PERFORMANCE OF INTERLIBRARY LOAN OPERATIONS IN NORTH AMERICAN RESEARCH AND COLLEGE LIBRARIES

EXECUTIVE SUMMARY

The ARL Interlibrary Loan and Document Delivery (ILL/DD) Performance Measures Study (the Study) was a two-year effort funded by The Andrew W. Mellon Foundation and undertaken by the Association of Research Libraries (ARL) in collaboration with the Council on Library and Information Resources (CLIR). The Study, which ran from July 1995 through December 1997, provided 1996 baseline data to enable librarians to identify and understand local performance of ILL/DD operations and compare the performance of their operations to other participants' operations. The project studied economic and non-economic indicators of ILL and DD services in 119 North American research and college libraries through analysis of four performance measures:

direct costs: Costs a library incurs to fill an ILL borrowing or lending request;

fill rate: Percentage of borrowing or lending requests successfully filled;

turnaround time: Number of calendar days to complete a borrowing request; and

user satisfaction: Level of user satisfaction with timeliness of the borrowing service, quality and completeness of material, and interaction with ILL staff.

A total of 97 research libraries, largely ARL members, participated in the Study. College libraries were represented by 22 members of the Oberlin Group, an informal affiliation of 74 highly competitive liberal arts colleges in the United States.

The Study tracked both borrowing and lending of returnables (books, microfilm, etc.) and non-returnables (copies of journal articles, etc.). The Study confirmed a wide range of performance among ILL/DD operations in research and college libraries. Overall, ILL/DD performance in college libraries was better than ILL/DD performance in research libraries. Summary analysis of findings includes the following averages:

	Research Libraries	College Libraries
Borrowing unit cost	$18.35	$12.08
Lending unit cost	$ 9.48	$ 7.25
Combined unit cost	$27.83	$19.33
Borrowing turnaround time	15.6 calendar days	10.8 calendar days
Borrowing fill rate	85%	91%
Lending fill rate	58%	65%
User satisfaction levels	94–97%	92–98%
Borrowing transactions	13,407	6,858
% Returnables	51%	39%
Lending transactions	27,722	5,109
% Returnables	36%	56%

There is a statistically significant difference in ILL/DD performance of research and college libraries. To the surprise and disappointment of the Study's Principal Investigator, analysis of more than 100 activities or characteristics did not find any cause of that difference.

Staff costs represented the major portion of the unit cost for a completed ILL transaction: 65% of the borrowing unit cost and 76% of the lending unit cost for research libraries, and 62% of the borrowing unit cost and 71% of the lending unit cost for college libraries.

The Study found a statistically significant relationship between the volume of lending and lending unit cost: As the volume of lending increases, the lending unit cost decreases. No similar statistically significant relationship was found for borrowing requests.

One objective of the Study was to identify and examine low-cost, high-performing ILL operations, defined as libraries falling in the top ten percent of each performance measure. Because of the small number of college libraries, examination of low-cost, high-performing operations was limited to research libraries. For **borrowing,** only one research library (Colorado State University) ranked in the top ten percent for low unit cost, high fill rate, and fast turnaround time. Five additional research libraries ranked in the top ten percent for two of the three performance measures.

The following characteristics are typical of high-performing borrowing operations.

Borrowing operations with **very low unit costs**:

- have decentralized their borrowing operations;
- have departments managed by support staff supervisors;
- make greater use of student assistants than most research libraries;
- use OCLC's ILL Fee Management to pay lending fees; and
- use management software to minimize paper files.

Borrowing operations with **very fast turnaround time**:

- require or encourage patrons to submit requests electronically;
- have activated OCLC's ILL Prism Transfer and/or FirstSearch-ILL link; and
- maximize use of Ariel document delivery software for Internet users, fax, commercial delivery carriers, and/or statewide delivery systems.

Borrowing operations with **very high fill rates**:

- have staff (professional or support staff) with extensive knowledge of collections, suppliers, lending policies, etc.;
- do not stop working on requests until the patron indicates the item is no longer needed; and
- do not limit the amount the library is willing to pay to obtain the item.

For **lending**, two research libraries (the University of Alberta and the University of Wisconsin–Madison) recorded high fill rates and low unit costs. Again, analysis of characteristics of high-performing lending operations reveals the following highlights.

Lending operations with **very high fill rates**:

- train students to specialize in retrieval from only one branch library;
- use Ariel, fax, and expedited delivery carriers for all shipments; and
- have liberal lending policies.

Lending operations with **very low unit costs**:

- have centralized their lending operations;
- do not use professional staff in non-supervisory roles;
- spend twice as much on a unit cost basis on hardware and software than do other research libraries;
- make extensive (and even experimental) use of technology; and
- accept credit cards for payment of lending fees.

Overall, the findings identified characteristics of low-cost, high-performing ILL/DD operations and provide an important input to the measurement of the overall performance of research and college libraries. In summary, findings of the ARL ILL/DD Performance Measures Study are intended to provide new opportunities for libraries to maximize access to remote resources while minimizing costs of such access.

March 1998

1 INTRODUCTION

Funded by The Andrew W. Mellon Foundation, the ILL/DD Performance Measures Study studied economic and non-economic indicators of ILL/DD services in 119 North American research and college libraries in order to identify low-cost, high-performing operations and to reconceptualize and improve ILL/DD services. Four performance measures were used: direct costs, fill rate, turnaround time, and user satisfaction.

1.1   BACKGROUND

Demand for interlibrary loan (ILL) and document delivery (DD) services is growing in libraries of all types and sizes. During the past decade, research library lending grew 61% and borrowing increased by 116%, with annual average increases measuring 5% and 8% respectively. In 1996, borrowing by the 120 members of the Association of Research Libraries (ARL) approached 2 million requests, and lending by ARL libraries topped 4.5 million requests.[1] Library administrators and ILL managers seek new strategies to accommodate this increased demand while continuing to provide a level of service acceptable to patrons.

The mission of the Association of Research Libraries is to shape and influence forces affecting the future of research libraries in the process of scholarly communication. One of ARL's eight strategic objectives is to describe and measure the performance of research libraries and their contributions to teaching, research, scholarship, and community service. ARL's Committee on Access to Information Resources helps the Association address strategies that make research information resources more accessible. In order to maintain and improve access to those resources, ARL undertakes activities to strengthen bibliographic tools, abstracting and indexing tools, user access, and physical and electronic access to information. Building on the Access Committee's recent focus of supporting resource sharing in an electronic environment, ARL launched the North American Interlibrary Loan and Document Delivery (NAILDD) Project[2] in 1993 and sought funding from The Andrew W. Mellon Foundation in 1995 to measure the performance of ILL operations in order to reconceptualize and improve ILL services.

The ILL/DD Performance Measures Study measured ILL services in research and college libraries in order to identify low-cost, high-performing operations. The Study is ARL's most recent effort to study ILL operations. For nearly three decades ARL has sponsored and supported studies to investigate interlibrary loan services in order to quantify costs, characterize operations, and, as articulated in 1971, develop **"an improved, adequate, and more equitable system."**[3] The Palmour Study, from which this quote was taken, was the first to calculate interlibrary loan costs in academic libraries on a national scale. That need, articulated nearly three decades ago, is still relevant today.

In 1988, Pat Weaver-Meyers and colleagues at the University of Oklahoma Libraries surveyed nearly 80 ARL members on workload and staffing trends in ILL departments. The results of that investigation were reported in an ARL Office of Management Services (OMS) Occasional Paper. (See Appendix M: Related Sources for complete references to the various publications referenced in this report.) The investigation reported a mean borrowing fill rate of 83% and a mean lending fill rate of 60%. The report discussed the effects of workload on fill rates and presented a formula to calculate total requests processed per full-time-equivalent (FTE).

In the early 1990s, ARL collaborated with the Research Libraries Group (RLG) and the Council on Library Resources (now the Council on Library and Information Resources, or, CLIR) on a study of the direct costs of ILL operations in research libraries. The 1992 ARL/RLG Interlibrary Loan Cost Study collected detailed information on direct costs for interlibrary loan transactions incurred by 76 research libraries. The report, *The ARL/RLG Interlibrary Loan Cost Study*, documented that a research library spent an average of $18.62 to borrow a book or receive a photocopy, and $10.93 to lend a book or supply a photocopy to another library.

Because the ARL/RLG ILL Cost Study measured only direct costs, it was not possible to judge the level of service research libraries were receiving or supplying for the combined sum of $29.55. By raising the awareness of the direct costs of providing interlibrary loan services, that study also raised many new questions. Research libraries had knowledge of direct costs of ILL services, but there were no data on the characteristics of low- or high-performing ILL operations. Nor did research libraries have data on other ILL performance measures, such as turnaround time or fill rate. Cost data were limited to research libraries; college libraries did not have data on the cost of an interlibrary loan transaction.

Finally, given the continued steep increase in the volume of ILL borrowing and lending, library administrators and ILL managers were anxious to reduce costs associated with ILL while expanding the level of service they provided. Interlibrary loan operations as they have been constituted for the past several decades are increasingly unable to respond to these growing service demands in a timely and cost-effective way.

---

[1] *ARL Statistics 1995-96.* (Washington, DC: Association of Research Libraries, 1997): 10-11.

[2] See Section 8.5 for additional information on the NAILDD Project.

[3] *A Study of the Characteristics, Costs, and Magnitude of Interlibrary Loans in Academic Libraries.* Prepared for the Association of Research Libraries by Westat Research, Inc. Compilers: Vernon Palmour, et. al. (Westport, CT: Greenwood Publishing, 1972): 6. Emphasis added.

Funded by The Andrew W. Mellon Foundation, the ILL/DD Performance Measures Study is the latest example of the interest ARL and The Mellon Foundation have in examining the economics of interlibrary loan services. The ILL/DD Performance Measures Study (the Study), a two-year effort undertaken by ARL in collaboration with the Council on Library and Information Resources, provided baseline data that allow librarians to identify and understand performance of ILL/DD operations and to compare the performance of their local operations to other participants. Begun in July 1995, the project studied economic and non-economic indicators of ILL/DD services in 119 North American research and college libraries through the investigation of four performance measures: direct costs, fill rate, turnaround time, and user satisfaction. Each measure is described more fully in Section 1.5. The Study was designed to place the cost of a filled interlibrary loan transaction into a larger context—that of overall performance of the service, thus the inclusion of fill rate, turnaround time, and user satisfaction. In addition, the Study provided additional comparative cost data for 63 libraries that participated in this Study and the 1992 ARL/RLG ILL Cost Study.

The ILL/DD Performance Measures Study defines interlibrary loan as the library process of obtaining or supplying books, microfilm, and other materials the lending library expects to have returned. Document delivery describes the process of obtaining copies of documents from libraries or document delivery suppliers or of supplying copies to other libraries. The Study tracked both borrowing and lending of books (returnables) and journal articles (non-returnables).

The Study also identified attributes of low-cost, high-performing ILL/DD departments in research libraries against which other research and college libraries can compare their local performance. Because analysis of the findings confirmed significant differences in research and college libraries' performance, this report presents separate aggregate data for the two groups of libraries. ILL operations in research and college libraries vary with the type and number of staff, the years of experience of that staff, the type of requests processed, and even the level and variety of technology available to ILL staff. Therefore, the performance ranges presented in this report may be more meaningful as a local comparison tool than the means or medians.

A word of warning: the findings presented in this publication should not be used as measures of library quality. In comparing any individual library to research libraries' or college libraries' means or medians, one must be careful to make such comparisons within the context of differing institutional and local goals and characteristics. Although the findings describe only the 119 participants in this Study, the findings are indicators of academic library trends for North America in general.

1.2   PROJECT OBJECTIVES

The ILL/DD Performance Measures Study defined five objectives:

1   Study six libraries that participated in the 1992 ARL/RLG ILL Cost Study to characterize the level of ILL performance provided by libraries with very high or very low unit costs.

2   Update ARL/RLG cost worksheets and collect current cost data.

3   Collect data on turnaround time, fill rate, and user satisfaction.

4   Collect data on research and college libraries.

5   Identify characteristics of low-cost, high-performing ILL operations.

1.3   METHODOLOGY

Because the Study was designed to build on and be compared, over time, to the ARL/RLG ILL Cost Study, ARL sought and received permission from James Michalko, President of the Research Libraries Group (RLG), to use the methodology and cost worksheets from that study as the basis for the current Study. The original survey instruments were developed by a six-member Task Force of the RLG Public Services Committee.[4] The RLG methodology itself had been adapted from a cost model developed by Stephen Dickson and Virginia Boucher.[5]

The ILL/DD Performance Measures Study was divided into two distinct sets of activities. The first, begun in summer 1995, examined in detail data of six participants from the ARL/RLG ILL Cost Study: three with very

---

4   Members of the RLG Task Force included Vivienne Roumani-Denn, University of California at Berkeley; Sharon Bonk, SUNY at Albany; Susanne McNatt, Princeton University; Patricia Renfro, University of Pennsylvania; Marilyn Roche, RLG; and N. J. Wolfe, New York University–Medical College.
5   Stephen P. Dickson and Virginia Boucher, "A Methodology for Determining Costs of Interlibrary Lending," *Research Access Through New Technology,* edited by Mary E. Jackson. (New York: AMS Press, 1989): 137-159.

high unit costs and three with very low unit costs. The purpose was to identify possible causal factors for those outlying costs. Section 2 of this report highlights the findings of that examination.

The second phase, begun in spring 1996, collected data on four performance measures from 119 North American research and college libraries by the use of survey instruments and questionnaires. Cost worksheets used for the ARL/RLG ILL Cost Study were reviewed and the staff worksheet was revised to collect data on staff for analysis by the Study's investigators, rather than having participants calculate and report staff cost. Instruments and worksheets were pre-tested by 17 members of the Big Twelve Plus consortium (formerly the Greater Midwest Research Library Consortium).[6] An electronic distribution list was established for all 119 participants and used as a means of sharing answers to general questions asked by individual participants. Participants received the first survey instruments in summer 1996. In May 1997, copies of the draft institutional reports were sent to all participants for review and data confirmation. Copies of the final institution-specific reports were mailed to participants in August 1997. This final report summarizes the results of both phases and concludes the Study.

1.4   STUDY TEAM AND ADVISORY COMMITTEE

A Study Team of two external consultants and a six-member Advisory Committee composed of directors of research and college libraries supported the Principal Investigator, Mary E. Jackson. Dr. Martin M. Cummings, Senior Consultant to the Council on Library and Information Resources, aided in the design and analysis of the Study, and commented on and critiqued the findings. Dr. Michael McPherson, then Dean of Williams College, served initially as the consulting economist. In May 1996, Dr. McPherson resigned as the Study's external consultant when he was appointed President of Macalester College. Dr. Bruce Kingma, Associate Professor, Department of Economics, and School of Information Science and Policy, University at Albany, replaced Dr. McPherson in July 1996.

The Advisory Committee provided assistance and guidance and served as links to several ARL Standing Committees. Advisory Committee members included:

Shirley Baker, Washington University in St. Louis (Chair); William Crowe, University of Kansas; Kent Hendrickson, University of Nebraska; Paul Kobulnicky, University of Connecticut; and William Studer, Ohio State University. In addition, Barbara Brown, Washington and Lee University, represented the Oberlin Group college libraries.

1.5   THE FOUR PERFORMANCE MEASURES: SUMMARY AND DEFINITIONS

Four measures were used to evaluate performance: direct costs, fill rate, turnaround time, and user satisfaction. Costs and fill rate were calculated using fiscal year (FY) 1995-96 data. In fall 1996, participants were asked to select between 125 and 150 borrowing requests from which turnaround time and user satisfaction were calculated; the actual number of forms and user surveys returned varied widely.

DIRECT COSTS: The first measure tracked direct costs associated with borrowing and lending transactions. To facilitate comparisons with the ARL/RLG ILL Cost Study, the same seven cost categories were used in this Study: staff, network/communication, delivery, photocopy, supplies, equipment, and (for borrowing) borrowing fees. As with the earlier study, the costs of general library functions, such as acquisitions, serials, or circulation, were not included, nor were costs of general library overhead, such as heat and utilities.[7] The Study did not track institutional costs of centralized invoice payment or the costs of users' time. Note also that cost data reported by the 13 Canadian participants are expressed in U.S. dollars. A conversion rate of 1.3613 Canadian dollars to one U.S. dollar was used.[8]

FILL RATE: The second measure calculated the percentage of borrowing and lending requests successfully filled based on annual borrowing and lending transactions received.

TURNAROUND TIME: The third measure calculated the length of time for a borrowing transaction to be completed (filled or unfilled). Turnaround time is the number of calendar days from the date the patron submitted an ILL request to the date the patron was notified of material availability or given a report of non-availability. The Study tracked turnaround time

---

[6] The 14 Big Twelve Plus members that participated in the pilot and full Study are noted in Appendix A.

[7] As was noted on page 2 of the *ARL/RLG Interlibrary Loan Cost Study*, collection development, acquisitions, and circulation are necessary preconditions for an ILL service and would be a cost to the library whether or not the library provided ILL services.

[8] The conversion rate was the same as used in the *ARL Statistics 1995-96*.

for borrowing only, based on returns from a requested sample size of 125 to 150 patron requests per participating library. **The scale and challenge of tracking turnaround time of lending operations was beyond the scope of this Study, but would be highly desirable to measure in a future investigation of interlibrary loan performance.** The Study calculated borrowing turnaround time using the following elements:

A Date on patron form
B Date accepted at service point
C Date processed by ILL staff
D Date sent to first supplier
E Date material received
F Date patron notified

USER SATISFACTION: The fourth measure tracked the satisfaction of individuals who submitted ILL/DD requests at their local library during the time frame of the Study. The results are based on the same small sample of ILL borrowing requests used to track turnaround time. The Study did not attempt to measure the satisfaction of individuals who did not use ILL/DD services during the Study's time period or who do not use ILL/DD services at all.

1.6 THE PARTICIPANTS

A total of 119 libraries participated in the Study, including 97 research libraries (89 university libraries and eight government or specialized non-university research libraries) and 22 college libraries. A roster of all participating libraries is included in Appendix A. Nearly two-thirds of the research library participants also participated in the 1992 ARL/RLG ILL Cost Study; those are also noted on the roster. The phrases

"research libraries" and "college libraries" signify libraries participating in this Study and do not extend to the larger membership of either ARL or the Oberlin Group unless otherwise noted.

One limitation of the 1992 ARL/RLG ILL Cost Study was that it calculated ILL costs for just research libraries. Some librarians speculate that ILL costs in college or public libraries are significantly less than costs reported for research libraries. To test this assumption, this Study was designed to measure performance in college libraries as well as research libraries.

The 97 research library participants are largely members of the Association of Research Libraries (ARL), a not-for-profit membership organization comprised of the largest research libraries in the United States and Canada. Most participants (86) submitted data from a central ILL department that provides borrowing and lending services for multiple branch libraries and special collections across a university or institution; the other 11 participants were branch or departmental libraries. Twenty-one of the 97 research library participants are private universities; 76 are public institutions. In all instances, ILL units provide services for undergraduate students, graduate students, faculty, and postdoctoral researchers. Six research libraries in the Study are non-university—government or private specialized libraries that provide ILL/DD services for a broad range of users.

The 22 college library participants are members of the Oberlin Group, an informal affiliation of 74 highly competitive liberal arts colleges in the United States. Oberlin Group members represent private institutions and their libraries provide ILL services to their primary clientele of undergraduate students and faculty. Figure 1 shows the geographic distribution of the two groups of participants.

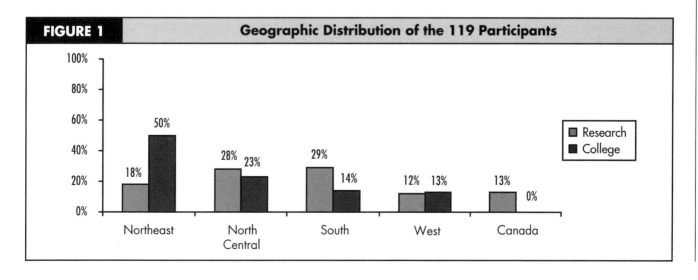

FIGURE 1 — Geographic Distribution of the 119 Participants

2 FOLLOW-UP EXAMINATION OF RESEARCH LIBRARIES WITH HIGH AND LOW UNIT COST ILL OPERATIONS

Detailed examination of six libraries from the 1992 study that reported very high or very low unit costs did not find any single factor but instead found several variables that may contribute to their unit costs: data accuracy, relative use of different staff categories, and use of technology.

2.1 BACKGROUND AND OVERVIEW

One aspect of the ILL/DD Performance Measures Study was to build on and expand the 1992 ARL/RLG ILL Cost Study. This expansion began by studying six libraries from the 1992 study with very high or very low unit costs, defined in this Study as "outliers." The purpose was to identify possible characteristics that contributed to the libraries' low or high unit costs. This, in turn, would contribute to the design for data collection in the new Study.

In discussion with the ILL/DD Performance Measures Study's external consultants, Dr. Michael McPherson and Dr. Martin Cummings, three libraries with high unit costs and three libraries with low unit costs were identified for in-depth study. Permission was sought and received from the directors of the six research libraries to have their 1992 data examined in greater detail in order to identify possible causal factors for their high or low unit costs.

The Principal Investigator visited all six libraries during the late fall of 1995 and early winter of 1996; members of the Study Team joined the Principal Investigator on some of the site visits. These visits validated data from the original submission and provided an opportunity for the Study Team to gain an overall sense of the operation. At each library, internal workflow and local policies were studied to see if local procedures and practices contributed to the high or low unit cost. All participants were asked to use the original cost worksheets to collect data on staff, network/communication, delivery, supplies, photocopy, equipment, and borrowing fees from the previous fiscal year. These updated unit costs would aid in understanding each library's current workflow and policies. Five of the six libraries completed that task.

2.2 SELECTING THE SIX LIBRARIES

The 1992 ARL/RLG ILL Cost Study reported borrowing and lending unit costs for 76 research libraries. Data from all participants were used to calculate the mean and median figures, but the charts and graphs included in that report presented ranges for only the middle 80% of participants. Data on libraries in the 0-10th and 90-100th percentiles were not included to assure confidentiality and to remove possible distortion provided by extreme values.

Findings from that study indicated that, for the middle 80% of participants, borrowing unit costs ranged from a low of $9.84 to a high of $30.27. For lending, unit costs ranged from $6.29 to $17.49. To aid in the selection of libraries with low and high unit costs, lists were prepared of libraries with borrowing unit costs of less than $9.84 or greater than $30.27, and lending unit costs of less than $6.29 or greater than $17.49. Since the majority of participants were U.S. universities, non-university and Canadian libraries were excluded from this phase to ensure comparisons of similar operations.

The Study Team selected six libraries from these lists. It is important to emphasize that the six libraries selected are not ones with the absolute highest, or lowest, unit costs, but are representative of libraries with very high or very low unit costs. Thus, the phrases "high unit cost" and "low unit cost" are to be interpreted as describing libraries with among the highest or lowest unit costs.

2.3 GENERAL CHARACTERISTICS OF THE SIX LIBRARIES

The libraries with high or low unit costs in the 1992 study share some common characteristics, but they also have many differences. Two are private and four are public universities, each representing different geographical regions of the U.S. They report a wide range of borrowing and lending transaction volumes. All six have centralized ILL operations serving multiple branch/departmental libraries. At the time of the original study, two had distinctly separate borrowing and lending operations, while four had one unit handling both borrowing and lending. All six are net lenders.

Only two of these six libraries offer electronic forms for patrons to submit requests. Most require patrons to fill out paper forms. All libraries use a variety of methods and messaging systems to send and receive requests. All participate in consortia, and most choose potential lenders based on consortial membership.

While the 1992 study did not measure fill rates, data from that study were used to calculate fill rates for the six libraries. Table 1 summarizes the average fill rates for the two groups of libraries.

Staff salaries accounted for three-quarters of the cost of an ILL transaction in all libraries studied in the 1992 ARL/RLG ILL Cost Study. Table 2 summarizes the

TABLE 1

Comparison of Mean Borrowing and Lending Fill Rates of the Six Libraries from the 1992 Study

	Borrowing Fill Rate	Lending Fill Rate
High unit cost libraries	87%	51%
Low unit cost libraries	80%	64%

2.4 CHARACTERISTICS OF RESEARCH LIBRARIES FROM THE 1992 STUDY WITH HIGH UNIT COST ILL OPERATIONS

The analysis of the three libraries revealed that many factors influence high unit cost operations; no single factor was identified as the cause of high unit cost in any library. This summary describes various borrowing and lending characteristics and does not attempt to draw conclusions. However, this section provides background on selected characteristics that many believe contribute to high unit cost operations. In combination with staffing levels and volume of transactions, these characteristics may contribute to a high unit cost operation. To assure confidentiality, the following summary excludes any data on the volume of activity processed as those numbers may permit readers to identify the institutions.

The three high unit cost libraries submitted accurate and detailed data. Cost worksheets were complete and included costs of staff with ILL responsibilities who work in other departments of the library, such as in reference or departmental libraries.

Two of the libraries require their patrons to come into the library to pick up photocopies. The third mails articles to patrons only if they have a campus address; if they live off-campus, they must come into the library to pick up photocopies. All three use the phone or mail to notify patrons to pick up materials. These practices take staff away from processing requests, which may result in lower productivity and increased costs. One library requires patrons to sign a form to "prove" that they received the material. Two libraries pass some or all of the lending charges on to local patrons, which

composition of borrowing and lending staff in the six ILL departments. Two differences are striking. First, although the percentage of professional staff is the same (10%), only the high unit cost operations employ professional non-supervisors (a librarian without supervisory responsibility) in the department. Second, low unit cost libraries use proportionately more students and fewer support staff than high unit cost operations.

This examination of the composition of staff in high and low unit cost operations suggests, at least in these six libraries, that costs may be driven by how much, or little, professional staff and student assistants were used. Unfortunately, this did not turn out to be the case for all 97 research libraries. Section 3.2.2 discusses the lack of a statistically significant relationship between use of different staff categories and unit cost. Therefore, in spite of staff salaries accounting for the major portion of unit costs, and despite the similarities of staffing characteristics of these six libraries, the Study did not find any statistically significant cause and effect between use of certain types of staff positions and unit costs.

TABLE 2	Staff Composition of the Six Libraries from the 1992 Study					
	High Unit Cost Libraries			Low Unit Cost Libraries		
	Low	Mean	High	Low	Mean	High
Professional supervisor	0%	5%	8%	7%	10%	15%
Professional non-supervisor	0%	5%	9%	0%	0%	0%
Support staff supervisor	0%	11%	29%	0%	9%	15%
Support staff	59%	69%	76%	35%	47%	55%
Students	8%	10%	12%	25%	34%	41%

may explain why articles are not mailed to patrons. In spite of the widespread installation of Ariel document delivery software for Internet users and fax machines that minimize the effects of distance on turnaround time, all libraries choose potential lenders based on geographic proximity. Two use document delivery suppliers, primarily because of the ease of requesting.

Two of the three libraries charge to lend materials; one accepts coupons; one does not. Both have manual invoicing systems and both impose lending fees to discourage other libraries from submitting excessive numbers of requests. One library has students carry lending forms to departmental libraries for retrieval and response; they do not fax requests to their branch libraries. One library concentrates on borrowing because they receive no "feedback" from their lending customers. Since they don't regularly communicate with libraries sending requests to them and therefore believe they are not in a position to encourage other libraries to use automated ILL messaging systems, this lending operation still receives most lending requests through the mail.

Two of the three had adequate space for staff and equipment; one operation was physically cramped. All three libraries have multiple, and sometimes duplicative, paper files; only one uses management software to track requests. All three libraries do not have complete control over their entire process; some must send their photocopying to a separate department, and none oversees mailroom functions.

One common feature of these three libraries is that they do not maximize technology. One library has one workstation per person, but the workstations are not networked or multitasked. Two do not use OCLC's MicroEnhancer, ILL Fee Management service, or custom holdings capabilities. Ariel and fax are available in two of the libraries, but are used for exceptional requests, not as a regular delivery method. Two noted problems with insufficient or inadequate printers.

The complex and perhaps inefficient workflow employed in one library may contribute to the three-week delay in sending borrowing requests to the first potential lender. This delay was observed in the course of a site visit made at one of the slowest periods of the year. It is unclear whether the three-week backlog is typical for this institution. A second example of how workflow might impact turnaround time became apparent on the site visit to another library. That library was two weeks behind in notifying patrons that their material had arrived.

All participants were asked to describe why their operations were high cost and to identify other potential causal factors not discovered by the cost study or site visits. One library believes that their level of staff, higher than average fringe benefit rate, and the length of service of some incumbents contributed to their high unit cost. Another thought the type of requests they received were more complicated than those received by other libraries. One library prided itself on a 96% borrowing fill rate, but did not know if their high fill rate directly contributed to their high unit cost.

Several subjective observations must be noted. All three libraries employ procedures used by libraries one and two decades ago: heavy reliance on paper forms, few automated internal procedures, and limited use of technology. Staff in all libraries appear to be more interested in maintaining current processes and procedures than investigating and implementing alternative ways of handling ever increasing workloads. Very few ILL staff, ILL managers, or their supervisors interviewed showed a particularly keen interest in technology.

Perhaps the most telling observation was the following comment: "The number one responsibility of ILL staff [in my library] was to do a perfect job." Attention to detail for all requests (such as checking the accuracy of the author and title of the article, or confirming availability before sending requests to potential lenders) may eliminate mistakes, but also contributes to a high unit cost. All three operations also display a staff-intensive customized approach to handling ILL requests. Each request is still reviewed by staff for completeness and accuracy before it is entered into an ILL system for processing. Most libraries with high volume ILL operations have found it more efficient to process requests on the assumption of accurate citations and manage the occasional exception only when it occurs.

2.5   CHARACTERISTICS OF RESEARCH LIBRARIES FROM THE 1992 STUDY WITH LOW UNIT COST ILL OPERATIONS

This section describes characteristics of three research libraries from the 1992 study with low unit cost ILL operations. As with the analysis of high unit cost operations, no single factor is identified as the cause of low unit cost. In contrast with high unit cost operations, all three low unit cost operations had major errors in data submitted on the 1992 worksheets. One library reported only staff costs, a fact that resulted in their unit cost being underrepresented by nearly 25%. That same library did not correctly report borrowing and lending staffing, which resulted in an inaccurate distribution of borrowing and lending costs. A second library significantly underrepresented some of their non-staff costs, particularly network and communication costs. That library also switched the percentage of time one individual worked in borrowing with that spent working in lending, further compounding inaccurate borrowing and lending unit costs. The third library incorrectly overreported staff costs and underreported borrowing and lending total transactions. Therefore, it is reasonable to conclude that all three libraries with low unit costs underrepresented actual costs.

However, there appears to be no connection between the underreporting of data and their status as low unit cost operations. Even when correct expenses and transaction volumes are used to recalculate unit costs, these three libraries still fall at the lower end of the range reported in the 1992 study. Thus, it is still informative to review the characteristics of their borrowing and lending operations, and their policies, workflow, and environment.

One library offers email forms to local patrons and has activated the OCLC FirstSearch-ILL link to permit patrons to submit requests electronically. The other two libraries require their patrons to submit paper forms in person. One library mails photocopies to patrons; the other two require patrons to come to the library to pick up articles.

Full-time staff, rather than students, retrieve materials in one of the libraries studied. Two of the libraries send materials that need to be photocopied to another department in the library, and although those costs were used to calculate their unit costs, it is not possible to determine whether use of copy service staff, rather than ILL staff, lowered staff costs in those two libraries.

All three low unit cost libraries have adequate space for staff and equipment. All three have multiple, and sometimes duplicative, paper files. Two do not use management software; one uses a locally-developed software to track requests.

All three libraries have centralized ILL operations. One library had separate borrowing and lending operations in 1992 which subsequently merged; the other two libraries combine borrowing and lending into one ILL unit. Like the high unit cost libraries, these three libraries underutilize technology. Most have Ariel and fax machines, but use them only for rush requests.

Other inefficiencies were identified in visits to low unit costs operations. One library feels a need to send many "conditional responses" on OCLC. A conditional response is a message to the borrower indicating why the lender can not fill the request. This policy decision to send many conditionals increases staff time spent on each request, which in turn impacts their unit cost. One operation has two separate lending streams in the office which results in duplicate files and inefficient use of staff.

One lending operation downloads new requests six times a day in the belief that most lending requests are filled or answered within 24 hours; that operation also does not charge to lend books. In another library with a low unit cost ILL operation, the borrowing operation reports an average turnaround time of four to five weeks. Staff take more than a week to send requests to the first lenders. It is discouraging to note that slow internal processing is common to the six libraries with high *and* low unit costs.

For the same reasons noted in the previous section, these three libraries were asked to speculate on why their operations were low-cost. Like responses from libraries with high unit costs, no conclusions could be drawn from these responses. One librarian worried that their worksheets were not reviewed by the library's business officer, and thus may have contained inaccurate data. A second librarian believed that their extensive use of students lowered their cost, but that speculation was not confirmed during analysis of their staff costs.

As with high unit cost operations, several subjective observations must be noted. The low unit cost operations are very traditional, with staff interested in maintaining the current processes. Staff exhibit little interest in changing procedures and workflow or exploring new technologies to reduce costs even further.

One comment from a staff member in a low unit cost library was most striking. The ILL manager indicated that the library director told their unit to "be thrifty." It is easier to pay $15, transaction-by-transaction, the ILL manager heard the director to say, than to establish deposit accounts or pay large net borrowing bills at the end of the fiscal year. This ILL department was instructed to use a specific document delivery supplier that billed on a transaction basis, but that supplier filled only 20% of the library's requests because the maximum cost the ILL department was permitted to pay was less than that supplier's average charge. If the library raised the minimum amount they were willing to pay from $7 to $12, over 80% of their requests could be filled by that document delivery supplier. In another effort to be thrifty, this library sent requests to libraries that did not charge lending fees, which resulted in significant staff time spent on locating no-fee libraries.

2.6   FINAL OBSERVATIONS

Detailed analysis of data from the 1992 study and on-site examination of workflow, procedures, and polices did not reveal any specific reasons why these six libraries had high or low unit costs. A few generalizations can be made with confidence. First, the three libraries with high unit cost operations were more accurate in reporting data, and, second, these libraries use higher paid levels of staff to process requests. Characteristics of high and low unit cost operations reveal several similarities that may argue for more comparable unit costs: all are net lenders, all underutilize technology and software, and all have procedures and policies that maintain the status-quo.

It is important to reiterate that this detailed examination did not find any single factor that caused any of these six libraries to have high or low unit costs. However, the investigation found several variables that may contribute to their unit costs: data accuracy, relative use of different staff categories, and use of technology. Because the ARL/RLG ILL Cost Study did not include other performance measures, such as fill rate or turnaround time, readers cannot conclude that research libraries with high unit cost ILL operations provide better service to local patrons and/or other libraries than research libraries with low unit cost ILL operations. Understanding how the unit cost of an ILL transaction relates to overall service performance was the goal of the second phase of this Study. This phase was launched with a renewed appreciation for the importance of data verification and with the expectation that the causal factors for different levels of performance would be found in indicators yet to be measured.

3   PERFORMANCE OF ILL/DD OPERATIONS IN 119 RESEARCH AND COLLEGE LIBRARIES IN 1996

For research libraries, staff costs account for 67% of the borrowing unit cost and 76% of the lending unit cost. For college libraries, staff costs account for 62% of the borrowing unit cost and 71% of the lending unit cost.

The Study found a statistically significant relationship between the voume of lending requests and lending unit cost: As the volume of lending increases, the lending unit cost decreases.

The Study confirmed that fill rates have not increased significantly over the past decade, despite increased availability of detailed serial holdings, current circulation information, and increased use of document delivery suppliers.

The average turnaround time for college libraries was nearly five calendar days faster than average turnaround time for research libraries.

Overall, ILL/DD performance in college libraries was better than ILL/DD performance in research libraries.

3.1 GENERAL OVERVIEW

The ILL/DD Performance Measures Study was completed in two distinct phases. Having completed the first phase of examining the six libraries with high and low unit costs, the Study entered the second phase and collected data on 1996 performance of interlibrary loan operations in North American research and college libraries using four performance measures. The purpose was to summarize current performance of ILL operations in these libraries and to identify characteristics of low-cost, high-performing ILL operations.

A total of 119 North American research and college libraries participated in this phase. The Study examined and reported performance of ILL/DD operations in research and college libraries as separate findings for two important reasons. First, there are significant differences in performance between the two types of libraries. Second, participants prefer to compare their own performance with operations in peer institutions.

Data from 97 research libraries were used to calculate aggregate data for research libraries; data from 22 college libraries were used to calculate aggregate data for college libraries. Table 3 summarizes the wide range of performance of ILL operations in research and college libraries.

To assure confidentiality of the institutions, data on libraries in the highest (90 - 100th percentile) and lowest (0 - 10th percentile) performance ranges are excluded from all figures and tables in this report.

TABLE 3	1996 Performance of ILL/DD Operations in Research and College Libraries	
ILL Volume & Performance Measures	97 Research Libraries	22 College Libraries
	10th to 90th percentile	10th to 90th percentile
Transactions		
Total	12,967 - 69,124	5,449 - 19,503
Borrowing	3,457 - 25,263	2,448 - 13,645
Lending	6,893 - 47,974	2,049 - 7,880
Unit Cost		
Borrowing	$9.76 - $27.84	$6.39 - $18.50
Lending	$4.87 - $16.34	$4.75 - $10.08
Fill Rate		
Borrowing	75% - 93%	85% - 97%
Returnables	71% - 97%	81% - 97%
Non-returnables	66% - 95%	72% - 97%
Lending	43% - 78%	54% - 87%
Returnables	41% - 79%	40% - 89%
Non-returnables	45% - 77%	33% - 87%
Turnaround Time		
Total	10.2 - 22.0 calendar days	6.7 - 16.9 calendar days
Returnables	10.4 - 25.8 calendar days	6.6 - 18.0 calendar days
Non-returnables	9.8 - 22.4 calendar days	6.3 - 16.6 calendar days
User Satisfaction		
Timeliness	88% - 99%	84% - 99%
Quality	94% - 100%	94% - 100%
Staff	85% - 100%	94% - 100%
User Paid	0% - 31%	0% - 28%
Amount Paid	$2.05 - $13.60	$0.28 - $14.00
Willing to Pay	$1.43 - $ 4.77	$0.89 - $ 3.32

Thus, all charts and scatter diagrams present findings for the middle 80% of each group of participants. Appendices B & C include a more detailed summary of the overall findings, including mean, median, 10th, 25th, 75th, and 90th percentiles. In this report, the terms "on average," "average," and "mean" are used interchangeably.

3.2 PERFORMANCE MEASURE: DIRECT COSTS

For research libraries, staff costs account for 67% of the borrowing unit cost and 76% of the lending unit cost. For college libraries, staff costs account for 62% of the borrowing unit cost and 71% of the lending unit cost. Rigorous regression analysis of staff positions and unit costs did not find any statistically significant relationship between the two. In other words, the Study did not find any cause and effect relationship between use of certain types of staff categories and higher unit costs, or non-use of certain types of staff categories and lower unit costs.

The Study found a statistically significant relationship between the volume of lending and lending unit cost: As the volume of lending increases, the lending unit cost decreases.

Seven categories were used to calculate the unit cost of an ILL/DD transaction: staff, network/communication, delivery, photocopy, supplies, equipment, and (for borrowing) borrowing fees. **The mean borrowing unit cost for research libraries is $18.35, and $12.08 for college libraries. The mean lending unit cost for research libraries is $9.48, and $7.25 for college libraries. Staff costs represent the single largest component of the unit cost for borrowing and lending in both research and college libraries.** Table 4 itemizes the mean borrowing unit cost by cost category and Table 5 presents a comparable summary for lending. Data are presented using the mean, or average, to facilitate comparison with the ARL/RLG ILL Cost Study. Selected tables and charts in this report also include median, or midpoint, data.

Section 3.6.1 summarizes the volume of ILL transactions filled by research and college libraries, and

TABLE 4	Mean Borrowing Unit Cost by Cost Category: Research and College Libraries			
	97 Research Libraries		22 College Libraries	
Staff	$12.07	66%	$ 7.44	62%
Network/communication	$ 2.24	12%	$ 1.60	13%
Delivery	$ 0.70	4%	$ 0.74	6%
Photocopy	$ 0.08	0%	$ 0.02	0%
Supplies	$ 0.16	1%	$ 0.14	1%
Equipment	$ 0.45	3%	$ 0.30	3%
Borrowing Fees	$ 2.65	14%	$ 1.84	15%
Total Unit Cost	$18.35	100%	$12.08	100%

TABLE 5	Mean Lending Unit Cost by Cost Category: Research and College Libraries			
	97 Research Libraries		22 College Libraries	
Staff	$7.23	76%	$5.17	71%
Network/communication	$0.35	4%	$0.39	6%
Delivery	$1.00	11%	$0.98	14%
Photocopy	$0.40	4%	$0.22	3%
Supplies	$0.16	2%	$0.15	2%
Equipment	$0.34	3%	$0.34	4%
Total Unit Cost	$9.48	100%	$7.25	100%

Appendix E includes a series of scatter diagrams comparing borrowing and lending unit costs with other performance measures. **The Study found a statistically significant relationship between the volume of lending and lending unit cost: As the volume of lending increases, the lending unit cost decreases. No similar statistically significant relationship was found for borrowing requests.**

3.2.1 Borrowing and Lending Unit Costs by Type of Participating Library

Participants in the Study included 89 university libraries, eight government or specialized non-university research libraries, and 22 college libraries. Given that the character and nature of the different subsets of participants vary, Table 6 compares mean borrowing and lending unit costs by type of participant. Section 5 provides a summary of the performance of the 13 Canadian participants and includes charts providing additional breakdown by type of participant.

3.2.2 Staff Costs

Because the largest single contributor to unit cost is staff salaries, a series of analyses on staff costs and composition of staff are presented in this section. It is important to remember that higher staff unit costs do not necessarily correlate with level of education or training of staff. Longevity of service may be among the factors that contribute to higher staff unit costs, but the Study did not ask participants to report employees' length of service.

Participants were asked to supply data on all library staff with interlibrary loan responsibilities and indicate whether they worked in the ILL unit or another department in the library. In research libraries, staff working

TABLE 6		
Comparison of Mean Borrowing and Lending Unit Costs by Type of Participating Library		
	Mean Borrowing Unit Cost	Mean Lending Unit Cost
97 Research libraries (U.S. & Canada)	$18.35	$ 9.48
84 U.S. research libraries	$16.67	$ 9.39
13 Canadian research libraries *	$28.81	$ 9.95
8 Non-university research libraries (U.S. & Canada)	$37.60	$14.56
22 U.S. College libraries	$12.08	$ 7.25

* All amounts expressed in U.S. currency.

in the ILL department account for 88% of total staffing used in the ILL process; in college libraries, staff in the ILL department account for 93%.

On average, research library participants assign borrowing-related tasks to staff outside the ILL unit nearly twice as often as college library participants. Likewise, research libraries assign lending-related tasks to staff in other departments of the library nearly five times as often as college library participants. Greater reliance on staff in other departments of the library may reflect the organizational complexity and/or multiple locations of research libraries. Figure 2 presents the mean

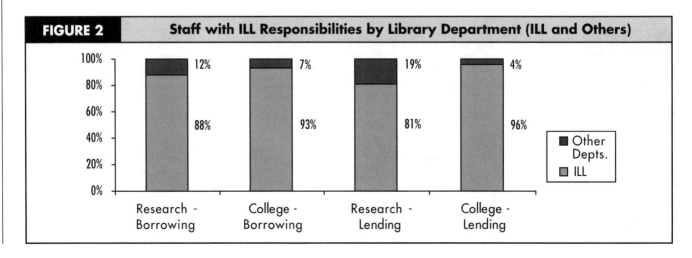

FIGURE 2   Staff with ILL Responsibilities by Library Department (ILL and Others)

TABLE 7	Mean Borrowing and Lending Staff Costs by Staff Category: Research Libraries			
	Borrowing		Lending	
	ILL Staff	Other Staff	ILL Staff	Other Staff
Professional supervisor	$ 1.88	$0.13	$0.73	$0.06
Professional non-supervisor	$ 0.62	$0.29	$0.21	$0.07
Support staff supervisor	$ 2.03	$0.17	$0.88	$0.15
Support staff	$ 5.44	$0.65	$3.29	$0.83
Students	$ 0.66	$0.20	$0.70	$0.31
Total	$10.63	$1.44	$5.81	$1.42

TABLE 8	Mean Borrowing and Lending Staff Costs by Staff Category: College Libraries			
	Borrowing		Lending	
	ILL Staff	Other Staff	ILL Staff	Other Staff
Professional supervisor	$1.92	$0.17	$0.98	$0.01
Professional non-supervisor	$0.54	$0.26	$0.08	$0.00
Support staff supervisor	$1.74	$0.01	$0.87	$0.00
Support staff	$2.03	$0.07	$1.87	$0.10
Students	$0.67	$0.03	$1.19	$0.07
Total	$6.90	$0.54	$4.99	$0.19

proportion of staff working in the ILL unit and in other departments in the library.

Staff costs as a percentage of total unit costs are similar in research and college libraries: 66% for research libraries and 62% for college libraries. However, the various staff categories used are quite different. Tables 7 and 8 present mean staff costs by staff category. Figures 3 and 4 compare the type of staff with ILL responsibilities by position category.

An examination of fringe benefit levels in the 20 libraries with the highest and lowest unit costs concluded that fringe benefits do not directly impact staff unit costs. The ten libraries with the highest staff unit costs have an average fringe benefit rate of 22%, while the ten libraries with the lowest staff unit costs report an average fringe benefit rate of 26.1%.

Just over a decade ago, Thomas Waldhart reviewed the research on the performance of interlibrary loan in the

United States. He examined a variety of institution-specific cost studies, and in discussing the cost study of 12 California State University libraries concluded that the "evidence suggests that the major contributor to the observed variation in the cost of interlibrary loan among different institutions may be the extent to which professional or clerical staff are used in interlibrary loan."[9] He called for further research to test his hypothesis that libraries in which the professional staff comprised a greater percentage of total ILL staff were ones with higher unit costs than libraries in which support staff predominated.

This ILL/DD Performance Measures Study examined staffing levels in detail, and did not find that the use or non-use of different types of positions contributed to the difference in unit costs.

For research libraries, the relationship between staff position categories and borrowing or lending unit costs was explored. Regression analysis is the statistical

[9] Thomas Waldhart, "Performance Evaluation of Interlibrary Loan in the United States; A Review of Research," *Library and Information Science Research* 7 (1985): 321-322.

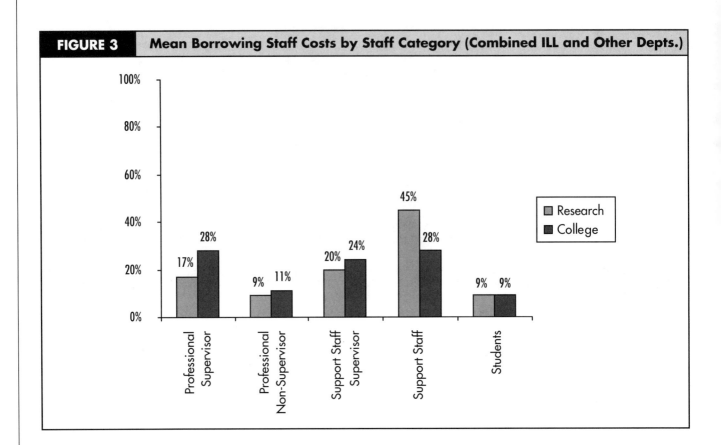

FIGURE 3   **Mean Borrowing Staff Costs by Staff Category (Combined ILL and Other Depts.)**

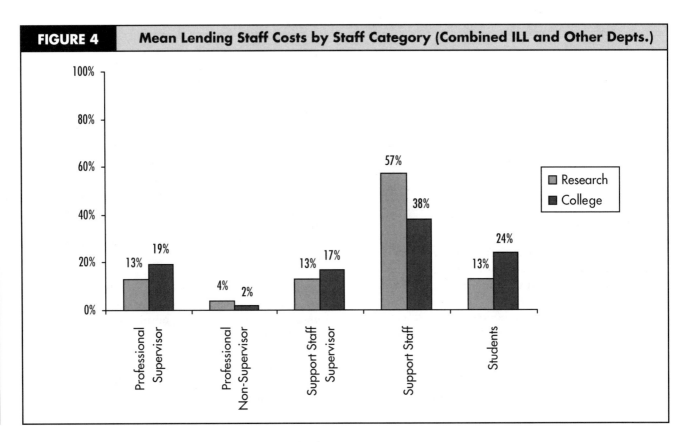

FIGURE 4   **Mean Lending Staff Costs by Staff Category (Combined ILL and Other Depts.)**

TABLE 9	Mean Borrowing and Lending Unit Costs by Region Adjusted for Cost of Living Differences					
Regions of the United States	Number of Libraries	Mean Cost of Living Index #	Mean Borrowing Unit Cost	Adjusted Mean Borrowing Unit Cost	Mean Lending Unit Cost	Adjusted Mean Lending Unit Cost
North Central	24	98.97	$13.27	$13.64	$ 6.75	$ 6.88
South	23	102.12	$16.16	$15.82	$10.35	$10.14
Northeast	15	136.96	$22.51	$16.99	$13.83	$10.01
West	10	107.72	$13.47	$12.63	$ 7.23	$ 6.69

tool used to tease out cause and effect relationships. A regression analysis was run on the various staff positions. **The analysis of staff costs by position classification confirmed that the variation in borrowing and lending unit costs is not a result of how much, or little, professional or support staff are used.**

Several strong positive correlations between unit costs and position types were found, suggesting that there may be a relationship. However, strong positive correlations do not confirm that one variable causes a change in a second. **The Study did not find any cause and effect between use of certain types of staff categories and higher unit costs, or non-use of certain types of staff categories and lower unit costs.**

This finding is both surprising and disappointing. It is surprising because, since staff salaries comprise two-thirds to three-quarters of the unit cost, there is a widely-shared assumption that the strategy to lower unit costs lies in reconfiguring the staff positions in the ILL department. It is disappointing because the investigators found no evidence of an ideal staffing combination that lowers unit cost. **Unit cost appears to be driven less by the type of staff deployed in ILL operations and more by how they work, the nature of their work, and the technology used to complete their work.** In summarizing the characteristics of low-cost, high-performing ILL/DD operations in research libraries, Section 7 of this report includes a number of recommendations for managing cost-effective ILL/DD operations. Therefore, this examination disproved a widely held belief that ILL operations with no professional staff (either as supervisors or non-supervisors) have lower unit costs than those with professional staff.

3.2.3 Regional Cost Differences in the U.S.

Staff salaries among Study participants differ in part because the cost of living varies from region to region within the U.S. and between the United States and Canada. The impact of regional salary variations was examined for the 72 U.S. research and college libraries for which cost of living data were available.[10] The cost of living index measures relative price levels for consumer goods and services in participating areas of the United States.

Table 9 presents mean borrowing and lending unit costs for the 72 U.S. research and college library participants located in cities or regions for which cost of living data were available. The table also shows borrowing and lending unit costs when adjusted for regional differences.

The adjusted mean unit costs for borrowing and lending minimize the impact of regional cost of living differences and show unit costs as if all regions of the United States had the same cost of living in terms of staff salaries or price of equipment, supplies, etc. Surprisingly, when cost of living differences are removed, the mean unit costs still differ by $4.36 for borrowing and $3.45 for lending. These variations are not attributable to regional salary variations, differential costs of purchasing equipment, supplies, etc., but reflect how staff are deployed and the organization of internal workflow and procedures.

3.2.4 Estimating Net Unit Costs

Although Study participants reported borrowing and lending reimbursements, this Study did not use those

---

[10] "No. 749: Cost of Living Index—Selected Metropolitan Areas: Third Quarter 1995," *Statistical Abstract of the United States 1996.* 116th ed. (Washington, DC: U.S. Bureau of the Census, 1996): 488–491.

TABLE 10 — Mean Borrowing and Lending Unit Costs, Reimbursements, and Net Unit Costs: Research Libraries		
	Borrowing	Lending
Mean Unit Cost	$18.35	$9.48
Mean Reimbursement	$ 0.42	$2.84
Net Unit Cost	$17.93	$6.64

TABLE 11 — Mean Borrowing and Lending Unit Costs, Reimbursements, and Net Unit Costs: College Libraries		
	Borrowing	Lending
Mean Unit Cost	$12.08	$7.25
Mean Reimbursement	$ 0.07	$0.60
Net Unit Cost	$12.01	$6.65

TABLE 12	Comparison of Mean Borrowing and Lending Unit Costs for Filled and Total Transactions			
	97 Research Libraries		22 College Libraries	
	Filled	Total	Filled	Total
Borrowing	$18.35	$15.60	$12.08	$10.99
Lending	$ 9.48	$ 5.50	$ 7.25	$ 4.71

sums to calculate borrowing or lending unit costs. As with the ARL/RLG ILL Cost Study, this investigation was designed to calculate total direct costs, not net costs. However, unlike the earlier study, this Study presents unit costs with and without reimbursements. Table 10 presents the average reimbursement and net unit costs for research libraries, and Table 11 presents findings for college libraries.

Borrowing reimbursements typically include money paid by patrons for some or all of the direct costs of an ILL transaction. Sources of lending reimbursements may include state funds to subsidize research library services for the citizens of the state and/or fees collected from and paid by the borrowing library for lending books, supplying photocopies, expedited processing, and/or postage/shipping. Based on the total borrowing and lending transactions generated by all ARL and Oberlin Group members (as detailed in Section 3.2.6), the Study estimates for all 120 ARL members a borrowing reimbursement of $833,000 and a lending reimbursement of $12,930,000. For the 74 Oberlin Group members, the Study estimates a total borrowing reimbursement of $27,000 and a total lending reimbursement of $207,000.

Tables 10 and 11 confirm that research libraries are reimbursed for a larger percentage of their lending costs than college libraries. Findings reported in these tables should be used with caution because the net cost represents only the final, direct cost to the library, not the total cost of completing an interlibrary loan transaction.

3.2.5 Calculating Unit Costs for Filled and Total Transactions

Calculating costs for any activity inevitably requires judgment about what and how costs are calculated. The 1992 ARL/RLG ILL Cost Study calculated unit costs using only filled transactions rather than total transactions, and some librarians felt this unfairly raised the unit cost of a filled request. However, as noted in the report of that study, filled transactions are the "products" of interlibrary loan; therefore, a comparison based only on filled transactions is similar to determining the unit cost of manufacturing based on finished goods, rather than the raw goods used to produce the finished goods. As that is still a valid argument, the current Study also used only filled transactions to calculate unit costs.

Libraries incur costs to process unfilled borrowing and lending requests and these costs were also collected in this Study. To get a sense of the variation in borrowing and lending unit costs if all transactions were used to calculate the respective unit costs, Table 12 compares the unit cost of a filled transaction with the unit cost of all transactions (filled and unfilled). Some librarians assert that handling an unfilled request is more costly than a filled request, and this is certainly true for some requests. However, this Study did not ask participants to track staff time spent on individual requests, so it was not possible to calculate the unit cost of an unfilled request.

3.2.6 Calculating Total ILL Expenditures by All ARL and Oberlin Group Libraries

In 1995/96, the 120 ARL member institutions generated 1,982,689 borrowing requests and filled 4,553,532 lending requests. Using mean unit costs for borrowing and lending ($18.35 and $9.48 respectively), the Study estimates that the 120 ARL member libraries expended $36,382,343 on borrowing activities, and $43,167,483 on lending, for a total of $79,549,826. Although the total is a significant dollar figure, it represents only 3.5% of 1995-96 total library expenditures, excluding materials costs incurred by ARL libraries.[11]

In 1995/96, the 74 college libraries that comprise the Oberlin Group generated 386,082 borrowing requests and filled 345,526 lending requests. Using borrowing and lending mean unit costs of $12.08 and $7.25 respectively, ARL estimates that the 74 Oberlin Group libraries expended a total of $4,663,871 on borrowing and $2,505,064 on lending. The $7,168,935 total represents 5% of total library expenditures by Oberlin Group libraries, again excluding material costs.[12]

On the basis of ARL data gathered over time,[13] one might expect the number of ILL transactions in research libraries to continue to increase at the current annual rate of eight percent for borrowing and five percent for lending. If this occurs, and assuming constant unit costs of $18.35 and $9.48 respectively, ARL member libraries would be spending about $53 million on borrowing and $58 million on lending, or a total of $111 million, by the year 2001.[14]

Interlibrary loan borrowing among the 74 Oberlin Group libraries increased 10.8% over the past five years while lending increased 7%. Assuming constant unit

costs ($12.18 and $7.25 respectively), in the year 2001 Oberlin Group libraries would be spending $11.2 million on ILL activities ($7.7 million on borrowing and $3.5 million on lending).

By using 1996 unit costs, the projections for ARL and Oberlin Group members assume actual unit cost savings over the next five years. If unit costs increase or the membership of either group increases, total expenditures will be even greater.

3.3 PERFORMANCE MEASURE: FILL RATE

The current Study confirms that ILL fill rates have not increased significantly over the past decade despite increased availability of detailed serial holdings, current circulation information, and increased use of document delivery suppliers.

Fill rate is the percentage of all borrowing or lending requests successfully filled. For each participant, borrowing and lending fill rates were calculated by dividing total filled requests by the total number of requests received in the fiscal year. Some participants provided the number of filled requests but were unable to provide the total number of requests received, either as lender or borrower. Aggregate fill rates were calculated using data from only those libraries that provided both filled and unfilled requests. Institution-specific fill rates were totaled and that sum averaged to result in the library fill rate reported in this Study. (However, the phrase *library fill rate* has been shortened in this report to *fill rate*.)

The range of fill rates, like the other performance measures, varies widely. **Borrowing fill rates for the middle 80% of research libraries ranged from 75% to 93%, with an average fill rate of 85%. Research libraries filled on average 83% of all returnable requests and 86% of all non-returnable requests submitted by local patrons. For lending, research libraries filled on average 58% of all incoming requests, with a range from 43% to 78%. Average lending fill rates for returnables and non-returnables were identical at 58%.** Table 13 summarizes the range of fill rates for research libraries. Note that research libraries with lending fill rates of 78% are exceptional; at the 90th percentile, only 10% of the Study participants perform at a higher level.

---

[11] *ARL Statistics 1995-96.* (Washington, DC: Association of Research Libraries): 37.

[12] Unpublished 1996 Oberlin Group data provided by Larry Frye, Wabash College.

[13] *ARL Statistics, 1995-96.* p. 11.

[14] It is important to remember that the 97 participating research libraries represent 80% of total ARL membership. In FY96, their transaction volume accounted for 63% of total ARL borrowing and 59% of total ARL lending. The 22 participating college libraries represent 30% of the total Oberlin Group membership (74), but they represent 44% of total Oberlin Group borrowing and 29% of all Oberlin Group lending.

TABLE 13	Range of Borrowing and Lending Fill Rates: Research Libraries			
	10th percentile	Mean	Median	90th percentile
Borrowing—Total	75%	85%	86%	93%
Returnables	66%	83%	86%	95%
Non-returnables	71%	86%	88%	97%
Lending—Total	43%	58%	57%	78%
Returnables	41%	58%	55%	79%
Non-returnables	45%	58%	56%	77%

TABLE 14	Range of Borrowing and Lending Fill Rates: College Libraries			
	10th percentile	Mean	Median	90th percentile
Borrowing—Total	85%	91%	92%	97%
Returnables	81%	90%	92%	97%
Non-returnables	72%	91%	93%	97%
Lending—Total	54%	65%	66%	87%
Returnables	40%	65%	68%	89%
Non-returnables	33%	63%	64%	87%

As shown in Table 14, college libraries overall recorded higher borrowing fill rates—ranging from 85% to 97%, with an average fill rate of 91%. College libraries successfully obtained 90% of all returnable requests and 91% of non-returnable requests for their patrons. On average, college libraries filled 65% of all lending requests, with a range from 54% to 87%. The average lending fill rate for returnables was slightly higher (65%) than for non-returnables (62%).

Borrowing and lending fill rates are not calculated in the same way. The borrowing fill rate is based on requests submitted by local patrons, not the number of libraries to which requests are sent. The lending fill rate is based on whether or not a library as a lender fills a specific request, not whether that request is ultimately filled. Many borrowing requests are sent to several libraries or document suppliers, each of which may respond negatively, before requests are ultimately filled, and, as a result, any individual library's lending fill rate is generally lower than its borrowing fill rate.

The Study did not ask participants to indicate reasons why their borrowing or lending requests were not filled. A borrowing library may cancel a request for a variety of reasons including: the item is owned locally;

the request could not be filled by the date the patron needed the item; correct bibliographic information about the item could not be found; no locations could be found; or the patron or library was unwilling to pay the fee charged by potential lenders.

Participants differed somewhat in how they counted borrowing requests for materials that are locally owned. Some counted those requests as filled requests since patrons were able to obtain the requested items. Others counted requests for locally owned materials as unfilled since they were not filled by other libraries. **A practical byproduct of the Study is a recommendation that, in the future, requests for "locally owned materials" should *not* be counted as filled borrowing requests. This recommendation is based on how high-performing borrowing operations count requests for materials locally owned.**

A lending library may not fill a request from another library for a number of reasons including: the item requested is not on the shelf; the lender charges a fee and the borrowing library was not explicit that it would pay the fee; or, by local policy, the item does not circulate to remote users (reference books or materials in special collections).

Slightly higher borrowing fill rates for non-returnables suggest that photocopies may be somewhat easier to obtain than books and other returnables, such as microfilm reels. This Study did not confirm that higher fill rates for photocopies are a direct result of increased availability and/or use of document delivery suppliers. Surprisingly, there is a slightly negative correlation between borrowing fill rates and use of document suppliers; that is, the more a library uses a document supplier, the lower the borrowing fill rate. However, through a regression analysis, the Study did not prove that use of document suppliers directly decreased the borrowing fill rate.

Findings from this Study did not settle the ongoing debate over which type of request is easier to process: a returnable or a non-returnable. Such noted authorities as Maurice Line in the United Kingdom suggest that requests for photocopies are much easier to fill than books; many ILL librarians are convinced otherwise. **Future investigations could explore why the fill rates for returnables and non-returnables vary, a level of investigation too detailed for this Study.**

Examining the "fail points" for unfilled requests may be more important than focusing on the absolute fill rate. Restrictive borrowing or lending policies may contribute to the overall fill rate and should be subject to further research.

The current Study confirms that ILL fill rates have not increased significantly over the past decade despite increased availability of detailed serial holdings, current circulation information, and increased use of document delivery suppliers. In 1989 Pat Weaver-Meyers reported the results of a survey of 76 ARL members on ILL workload and staffing patterns. The average borrowing fill rate was 83%, only one percentage point lower than the results of the current Study. In 1989 the average lending fill rate for research libraries was 60%, two percentage points higher than the results of this Study. Although virtually all ILL operations have much easier access to current information on holdings and circulation availability than they had a decade ago, this Study cannot offer insight why the average borrowing and lending fill rates for research libraries have remained virtually unchanged over the past decade.

Several recent studies report fill rates comparable to the findings of this Study. Data from the OCLC ILL System for 1995/96 supplied to ARL by OCLC also confirm lending fill rates well within the norm for this Study. For example, according to OCLC's data, the main ILL departments in this Study were able to fill 48% of all incoming lending requests. Note that OCLC counts a request as unfilled if not filled by any lender in the lending string. However, some of these unfilled requests were re-initiated and eventually filled, counted by OCLC one or more times as an unfilled request and finally as a filled request. These result in a somewhat lower fill rate than the level determined in this Study. OCLC also reported an overall borrowing fill rate of 78%, again reflecting the OCLC counting method but still comparable to the results of this Study.

The Research Libraries Group (RLG) has examined why requests cannot be filled. Unlike OCLC, the RLIN ILL system permits lenders to indicate reasons why they are unable to fill requests. In early 1997 RLG staff scanned unfilled ILL requests and concluded that the most common reason for non-supply is *lack*, i.e., the library owns the serial title, but not the needed issue. *Other* is the second most common reason, followed closely by *in-use* and *not-on-shelf*.[15]

Several studies report institution-specific fill rates. One such example is Christine Guyonneau's examination of unfilled lending requests at the University of Indianapolis Library. In a late 1980s study, she concluded that the three most common reasons her library could not fill lending requests were: 1) item not on shelf; 2) serial title owned, but not the particular issue; and 3) item non-circulating.

Why Requests Fail: Interlibrary Lending and Document Supply Request Failures in the UK and Ireland reported results of a study conducted by David Parry for the Circle of Officers of National and Regional Library Systems (CONARLS). The 1997 study sought to identify and measure various types of failures by sampling ILL request cancellations from a variety of types of libraries. The project also examined requests unfilled by the British Library Document Supply Centre (BLDSC). Fifteen (15) university libraries were studied, but no college libraries. The most common reason for cancellation was "verification failure" (26%), followed by "no locations found" (18%). Generally, university libraries send requests to BLDSC without verification, a process quite different from that followed in North America, and perhaps a contributing factor to the difference in

---

[15] It is important to note that the RLIN and OCLC ILL systems count ILL requests differently. **Reaching national agreement on counting strategies for filled and unfilled requests generated on all online ILL systems would enable ILL managers to use statistical reports generated by those systems with confidence that ILL requests were being counted consistently.**

the most frequently cited reason for failure. Also applicable to North American libraries may be a mindset expressed in the report's concluding statement: "Some things, you just aren't going to get."[16]

In a May 1989 report of a project funded by the Australian Council of Libraries and Information Services, Colin Taylor included several recommendations for improving ILL performance for Australian libraries. **He recommended that libraries with a "first attempt success rate" below 80% or "second attempt success rate" below 90% should review their procedures to improve performance.** He noted an overall borrowing fill rate of 94% (97% for non-returnables and 91% for returnables) and recommended that libraries should measure their borrowing fill rate on a regular basis and should target a fill rate of not less than 95%. **The targets recommended by Taylor, if also pursued by North American libraries, would significantly improve the performance of ILL/DD operations.**

3.4   PERFORMANCE MEASURE: TURNAROUND TIME

The Study found quite a range of turnaround time averages. For research libraries, average turnaround time ranged from 10.2 to 22.0 calendar days. For college libraries, average turnaround time ranged from 6.7 to 16.9 calendar days. Tables 15 and 16 summarize turnaround time for research and college libraries respectively.

Libraries receiving fewer than 25% of their requests within seven days and fewer than 80% within four weeks should review their procedures to see how performance can be improved.

Turnaround time is the number of calendar days taken to complete a borrowing request. In the 1996 fall term, each participating library was asked to select in a random manner between 125 to 150 borrowing requests from which turnaround time and user satisfaction would be calculated. Actual sample sizes ranged from 18 to 396 requests. The consulting economist confirmed that a sample size of 125 to 150 requests, although small, would still produce valid results. Participants were asked to record seven dates, beginning with the date the patron initiated the request and concluding with the date the ILL unit notified the patron of availability or non-availability. The specific dates included:

A   Date on patron form
B   Date accepted at service point
C   Date processed by ILL staff
D   Date sent to first supplier
E   Date material received
F   Date patron notified

Turnaround time is reported in calendar days, not working days, to reflect turnaround time as viewed by the patron. **The Study did not measure turnaround time for non-returnables in hours, but future investigations may benefit from tracking non-returnables in hours as well as days, given increased use of electronic delivery technologies and/or access to full-text or full-image documents.**

The Study found quite a range of turnaround time averages. For research libraries, average turnaround time ranged from 10.2 to 22.0 calendar days. For college libraries, average turnaround time ranged from 6.7 to 16.9 calendar days. Tables 15 and 16 summarize turnaround time for research and college libraries respectively.

The Study measured separate turnaround times for returnables and non-returnables. Research libraries recorded a range of 10.4 to 25.8 days for returnables, with an average of 16.9 days. Non-returnable requests ranged from 9.8 to 22.4 days, with an average of 14.9 days. On average, photocopies arrived two days before books but still slower than one might expect given increased availability of document suppliers and use of fax and Ariel as expedited delivery methods. The Study did not ask participants to record the method by which items tracked in the sample were received, but given responses to questions in the General Characteristics Questionnaire, it is possible to speculate that widespread use of commercial delivery services such as UPS and/or state couriers may minimize the difference between returnables and non-returnables.

For returnables, research libraries averaged 3.5 days to send a loan request to the first lender, 13 days to receive the item, and half a day to notify the patron. For non-returnables, research libraries took, on average, four days to send a photocopy request to the first lender/supplier, 11 days to receive the article, and half a day to notify the patron.

Average turnaround time for college libraries is five days faster than the average turnaround time for

TABLE 15	Range of Turnaround Time in Calendar Days: Research Libraries			
	10th percentile	Mean	Median	90th percentile
Total	10.2 days	15.6 days	14.9 days	22.0 days
Returnables	10.4 days	16.9 days	16.3 days	25.8 days
Non-returnables	9.8 days	14.9 days	13.8 days	22.4 days

TABLE 16	Range of Turnaround Time in Calendar Days: College Libraries			
	10th percentile	Mean	Median	90th percentile
Total	6.7 days	10.8 days	9.5 days	16.9 days
Returnables	6.6 days	11.4 days	10.9 days	18.0 days
Non-returnables	6.3 days	10.4 days	8.4 days	16.6 days

research libraries. Turnaround time for returnables ranged from 6.6 to 18.0 days, with an average of 11.4 days. The range for non-returnables was 6.3 to 16.6 days, with an average of 10.4 days. On average, college libraries took 2.5 calendar days to send a loan request to the first lender, nine days to receive the item, and half a day to notify the patron. For non-returnables, college libraries took 3.5 days to send a photocopy request to the first lender/supplier, seven days to receive the article, and half a day to notify the patron.

Average turnaround time may be skewed by requests that are completed very quickly or very slowly. Therefore, the Study also examined the cumulative percentage of requests received within defined periods of time. Within seven days, research libraries obtain just less than one-quarter of all requests for returnables and one-third of all requests for non-returnables. College libraries obtain about one-half of both types of requests in the same time frame. Table 17 presents the ranges for research libraries and Table 18 does the same for college libraries.

TABLE 17	Cumulative Mean Borrowing Turnaround Time: Research Libraries		
	All Requests	Returnables	Non-returnables
0-3 calendar days	8%	6%	9%
0-7 calendar days	27%	22%	30%
0-14 calendar days	61%	57%	64%
0-21 calendar days	80%	77%	83%

TABLE 18	Cumulative Mean Borrowing Turnaround Time: College Libraries		
	All Requests	Returnables	Non-returnables
0-3 calendar days	16%	16%	16%
0-7 calendar days	44%	39%	49%
0-14 calendar days	75%	73%	77%
0-21 calendar days	91%	90%	91%

Only *completed* borrowing requests were used to calculate turnaround time, and thus, average turnaround time is underrepresented. Requests in process at the end of the sample period were excluded from the calculation of turnaround time. If all sample requests were completed and then used to calculate turnaround time, average turnaround time for both groups of libraries would increase by approximately three days.

This Study tracked turnaround time from the perspective of the borrower but did not ask participants to record the total number of libraries or suppliers to which requests were sent. As a result, the Study does not report turnaround time for individual lenders or document suppliers. Data from the OCLC and RLIN ILL systems suggest that requests are sent to an average of two libraries before they are filled. Therefore, it is important to remember that the turnaround time reported in this Study includes the time it took the first library to forward the request to another potential lender/supplier. **Overall, turnaround time will be faster if lenders check their shelves only one time and then forward requests to the next library/supplier rather than re-checking shelves over the course of several days (and not finding the needed item on subsequent searches) before forwarding unfilled requests to other libraries.**

Other turnaround time studies confirm the time it takes for an ILL request to be filled. A 1996 study of turnaround time for libraries using the WLN ILL system reported an average of 11 days from the day the request is routed to the library that supplied the item until the item is received, slightly longer than the comparable subset of this Study's turnaround time.[17]

However, the findings of this Study are not comparable to the turnaround time promised by most document delivery suppliers. Many document suppliers advertise 48 hour processing, and many meet this goal. However, this definition of turnaround time cannot be compared to the borrowing library's turnaround time because two different definitions are used. Document delivery suppliers define turnaround time as suppliers, not requesters. They measure from the date they receive the request to the date they ship the item, and do not include delivery time to the requester/borrower. A supplier's definition of turnaround time is a portion of

one of six subsets of a library's overall borrowing turnaround time as defined by this Study. In order to make a fair comparison of document delivery services with the equivalent subset in this Study, a library would have to compare the number of days from the date of submission to the document supplier to the receipt of the article from the supplier, or between steps "D" (date sent to first supplier) and "E" (date material received) as defined previously in this section. The library would also need to account for any delays caused by other potential libraries or suppliers if they do not send the request directly to the supplier.

The library literature includes numerous studies that compare turnaround time of document delivery suppliers and libraries.[18] These studies report average turnaround times of between ten and 14 days; however, some studies measured turnaround time from the point the request was sent to the supplier, or counted working days rather than calendar days.

Colin Taylor's 1989 Australian study reported comparable turnaround times: 5% within one day, 21% within seven days, 77% within 28 days, and noted that overall supply time "was not particularly impressive." **Taylor recommended that libraries receiving fewer than 25% of their requests within seven days and fewer than 80% within four weeks should review their procedures to see how performance can be improved, a recommendation that the present Study endorses for North American libraries.**

3.5   PERFORMANCE MEASURE: USER SATISFACTION

It is possible that high satisfaction ratings reflect users' satisfaction with past experiences rather than specific requests submitted during the sample period.

User satisfaction is not a measure of the quality of the service. Users may be simply too grateful to discriminate between acceptable and unacceptable service.

Users for whom current ILL service is too slow have often found alternative options to fill their information needs.

---

[17] Kathy Forsythe, "WLN Online System . . . How it Works For You," *WLN Participant* 15 (Winter 1996): 7.

[18] See, for example: Janet Hughes, "Can Document Delivery Compensate for Reduced Serial Holdings? A Life Sciences Library Perspective," *College & Research Libraries* 58 (September 1997): 421-431; Thomas L. Kilpatrick and Barbara G. Preece, "Serials Cuts and Interlibrary Loan: Filling the Gaps," *Interlending & Document Supply* 24 (1996): 12-20; Kathleen Kurosman and Barbara A. Durniak, "Document Delivery: A Comparison of Commercial Document Suppliers and Interlibrary Loan Services," *College & Research Libraries* 55 (March 1994): 129-139; and Wayne Pedersen and David Gregory, "Interlibrary Loan and Commercial Document Supply: Finding the Right Fit," *Journal of Academic Librarianship* 20 (November 1994): 263-272.

User satisfaction is defined as the extent to which current users of ILL borrowing services are satisfied with the service they received during the Study's time frame. The Study did not attempt to measure the satisfaction of individuals who did not use ILL during the Study period or who do not use ILL at all.

The Study's Advisory Committee confirmed the importance of surveying current interlibrary loan users about their level of satisfaction with the service. Based on the additional expense and time required, a decision was made not to undertake a comprehensive and detailed user satisfaction survey, such as the SERVQUAL instrument used by François Hébert to measure service quality from the perspective of users of ILL services in Canadian public libraries or by Danuta Nitecki to measure the views of ILL users at the University of Maryland Libraries.

Instead, the sample of 125 to 150 borrowing requests per library used to track turnaround time was also employed to measure user satisfaction. Again, the consulting economist confirmed that this sample size, although small, would produce valid results. Participants were asked to include a brief questionnaire with each ILL item received (or report of unavailability) in the sample. Patrons receiving questionnaires were asked to respond to the following questions:

1 Did the item (or negative response) arrive within an acceptable time frame, or by the date by which you indicated you needed the request? If no, why?

2 Was the quality of the photocopy acceptable or were all volumes of the book title or microform reels supplied?

3 If the request was not filled, do you believe the ILL staff did all they could to obtain the item?

4 Did you have to pay for this request? If yes, how much? If no, how much would you be willing to pay for this request?

Patrons were asked to return questionnaires in sealed envelopes to the ARL office or to their library's ILL department. Mean user response rate was 51%, and, with highly variable response rates, data on user satisfaction should be used with caution. Response rates for the participants that completed this phase are included in Appendix A.

The Study found high levels of user satisfaction. Findings for research library participants are summarized in Table 19, and Table 20 presents findings for college libraries.

TABLE 19	Range of User Satisfaction: Research Libraries			
	10th percentile	Mean	Median	90th percentile
Timeliness	88%	94%	95%	99%
Quality	94%	97%	97%	100%
Staff	85%	95%	96%	100%
Users paid	0%	8%	2%	31%
Amount paid	$2.05	$6.95	$4.75	$13.60
Willing to pay	$1.43	$2.71	$2.25	$ 4.77

TABLE 20	Range of User Satisfaction: College Libraries			
	10th percentile	Mean	Median	90th percentile
Timeliness	84%	92%	95%	99%
Quality	94%	98%	98%	100%
Staff	94%	98%	100%	100%
Users paid	0%	10%	2%	28%
Amount paid	$0.28	$6.50	$5.24	$14.00
Willing to pay	$0.89	$2.15	$1.96	$ 3.32

Fewer than ten percent of all research libraries asked their users to pay for ILL requests, and the average charge was just under $7.00. ILL patrons who were not charged were asked how much they were willing to pay for an ILL request: research library patrons would pay between $1.43 and $4.77, and college library patrons were willing to pay from $0.89 to $3.32. Using an average of 10 pages per article and an average photocopy charge of $0.10 per page, the average fee a patron is willing to pay ($2.15 or $2.71) is double the patron's cost of making a photocopy at the local library ($1.00). However, these amounts are still significantly less than any document delivery supplier's average charge of $7.50 to $15.00.

Several correlations were run to see if research library users who paid for articles expressed higher satisfaction with the service as measured by turnaround time, quality of materials received, or interaction with staff. Weak positive correlations were found for all three, with the strongest correlation (+0.13) between payment and interaction with ILL staff. This Study did not establish that users who pay for ILL services, regardless of the amount they pay, are significantly more satisfied than users who are not asked to pay.

It is possible that high satisfaction ratings reflect users' satisfaction with past experiences rather than specific requests submitted during the sample period. User satisfaction is not a measure of the quality of the service. Patrons may be simply too grateful to discriminate between acceptable and unacceptable service. Users for whom current ILL service is too slow have often found alternative options to fill their information needs. Therefore, the findings of the user satisfaction measure should be used with caution. **Additional research should identify a group of potential users from high-performing borrowing operations and explore why they do not use ILL services.**

3.6 GENERAL CHARACTERISTICS OF ILL OPERATIONS

Decentralized borrowing results in a lower unit cost, faster turnaround time, and a slightly higher fill rate. However, economies of scale are more evident with centralized lending because centralization results in lower unit costs and higher fill rates.

For the group of libraries that receive more than 20% of their photocopy requests from document suppliers, there is a weak positive correlation between use turnaround time and use of document suppliers. That is, the more requests filled by document suppliers, the slower the turnaround time. This finding contradicts the primary reason why many ILL managers use document delivery suppliers—faster turnaround time.

The Study asked approximately 50 questions about general characteristics of interlibrary loan operations. The General Characteristics Questionnaire is included in Appendix G. Responses provide an overview of the current structure, organization, composition, and service policies of the 119 participants. This section highlights some of the more noteworthy findings.

3.6.1 Volume of Borrowing and Lending

In FY96, the year studied, the average number of filled borrowing transactions totaled 40,571 for research libraries and 11,968 for college libraries. Table 21 presents the range of total filled (borrowing and lending) transactions.

Table 22 itemizes total ILL transactions by borrowing and lending. The patterns for research and college libraries are notably different. For every filled borrowing request, a research library filled two lending requests. The pattern in college libraries is reversed: borrowing materials for local patrons represented 57% of total traffic, and lending, 43%.

TABLE 21	Range of Total Filled (Borrowing and Lending) Transactions: Research and College Libraries			
	10th percentile	Mean	Median	90th percentile
Research libraries	12,967	40,571	30,131	69,124
College libraries	5,449	11,968	9,912	19,503

TABLE 22

Proportion of Borrowing to Lending Requests: Research and College Libraries

	Research Libraries	College Libraries
% borrowing	33%	57%
% lending	67%	43%
Total	100%	100%

The 97 participating research libraries represent 80% of total ARL membership. In FY96, their ILL transaction volume accounted for 63% of total ARL borrowing and 59% of total ARL lending. The 22 participating college libraries represent 30% of the total Oberlin Group membership (74), but 44% of total Oberlin Group borrowing and 29% of total Oberlin Group lending. Applying the findings from either group to their respective aggregate memberships should be done with caution.

3.6.2 Proportion of Returnables to Non-Returnables

The type of ILL transactions processed by research libraries has not changed in the past decade. The average proportions of returnables and non-returnables for borrowing and lending in research libraries are identical to the proportions reported in the 1992 ARL/RLG ILL Cost Study. Returnables (or loan requests) are books, microfilm reels, or other materials the lender expects to have returned. Non-returnables (or photocopy requests) are copies of journal articles, papers in conference proceedings, or copies the library or supplier does not expect to have returned.

On average, research library borrowing was split evenly between returnables and non-returnables. Research library lending was one-third returnables and two-thirds non-returnables. Table 23 summarizes research library borrowing and lending by type of request.

College libraries process very different proportions of returnable and non-returnable requests. On average, college library borrowing was 39% returnables and 61% non-returnables. College library lending was more evenly split at 56% returnables and 44% non-returnables. Table 24 summarizes college library borrowing and lending by type of request.

The Study did not ask participants to describe why their borrowing or lending reflected a particular proportion of returnables to non-returnables. The more extensive and retrospective journal collections held by research libraries may contribute to the higher proportion of supply of non-returnables. College libraries, on the other hand, obtain more non-returnables for their patrons, in part because college library journal collections are smaller than those maintained by research libraries. In FY96, the average number of serial titles currently received by ARL libraries was 21,107, while the average number of periodical and serial titles currently received by Oberlin Group libraries was 4,212.

TABLE 23   Range of Returnables to Non-Returnables: Research Libraries

	Borrowing				Lending			
	10th	Mean	Median	90th	10th	Mean	Median	90th
Returnables	43%	51%	46%	49%	60%	36%	45%	40%
Non-returnables	57%	49%	54%	51%	40%	64%	55%	60%

TABLE 24   Range of Returnables to Non-Returnables: College Libraries

	Borrowing				Lending			
	10th	Mean	Median	90th	10th	Mean	Median	90th
Returnables	37%	39%	37%	43%	65%	56%	54%	57%
Non-returnables	63%	61%	63%	57%	35%	44%	46%	43%

3.6.3   Requests per FTE

Like other performance measures, the quantity of borrowing and lending requests handled by ILL staff varies widely. ILL staff in participating libraries are responsible for a range of tasks—from receiving requests, searching and initiating requests, maintaining files and invoicing, retrieving materials, to photocopying and wrapping/unwrapping. In some libraries, these tasks are handled by staff in other departments such as reference, photocopy services, or the mailroom.

The range of requests processed per person confirms that many factors contribute to how many total requests an individual can process in one year. In addition to the number and types of tasks assigned to ILL staff, the number of ILL requests an individual is able to process may be influenced by the number of staff in the ILL department, the type of staff positions, ease of access to equipment, and internal procedures and workflow.

Recognizing that ILL staff have a wide range of processing responsibilities, the Study calculated the average number of total ILL requests processed per FTE. For the 97 research libraries, total borrowing requests per FTE range from 574 to 101,728, and 1,236 to 47,348 for total lending requests per FTE. For the 22 college libraries, average requests per FTE range from 2,505 to 6,397 for borrowing, and 3,277 to 24,869 for lending.

Because of the variability in tasks performed by ILL staff, it is difficult to calculate precisely how many requests an individual can handle in one year. Table 25 presents the mean number of total (filled and unfilled) requests processed per ILL FTE by different subgroups of participants. It is interesting to note that the high-performing borrowers processed the largest number of borrowing requests per FTE, but high-performing lenders actually processed slightly fewer lending requests per FTE than the high-performing borrowers. Because of the factors noted above, readers are cautioned not to use the findings presented in this table in isolation from the other Study findings.

3.6.4   Organization and Administration

On average, research libraries have 2.5 ILL processing units and college libraries have one ILL unit. The variance is probably due to the differing size and composition of the two types of libraries. On average, an ILL unit in a research library serves seven branch/departmental libraries, whereas an ILL unit in a college library serves two branch/departmental libraries.

Although ILL operations in the majority of research libraries are centralized, medical, law, and some departmental or branch libraries usually maintain separate ILL units. Since most research libraries have medical and/or law libraries, this may explain the larger number of ILL units in research institutions.

Over 90% of borrowing and lending operations in participating research libraries and 95% of those operations in participating college libraries are centralized. In the research libraries studied, only nine borrowing and eight lending operations are decentralized. Only one borrowing operation and one lending operation is decentralized in the college libraries studied.

TABLE 25	Comparison of Mean Total Requests Processed per FTE by Various Subgroups of Participants					
	Borrowing			Lending		
	Mean Req./ FTE	Mean # Staff	Median # Staff	Mean Req./ FTE	Mean # Staff	Median # Staff
97 research libraries	4,821	4.06	4.00	8,977	6.01	4.20
22 college libraries	4,397	1.81	1.38	6,899	1.28	1.12
13 Canadian research libraries	2,517	2.80	2.65	5,721	8.74	3.20
84 U.S. research libraries	5,125	4.23	4.12	9,449	5.55	4.25
5 borrowing operations in research libraries with the lowest unit costs	5,361	4.49	4.83	10,127	5.19	4.05
5 lending operations in research libraries with the lowest unit costs	3,929	6.43	6.30	9,352	9.58	9.94

TABLE 26	Comparison of Mean Borrowing and Lending Performance of Centralized, Decentralized, and All Research Libraries ILL Operations		
	9 Decentralized ILL Operations	88 Centralized ILL Operations	97 Research Libraries
Borrowing			
Cost	$17.24	$23.16	$18.35
Turnaround time	13.1 days	17.6 days	15.6 days
Fill rate	87%	83%	85%
Lending			
Cost	$13.57	$6.74	$9.48
Fill rate	57%	45%	58%

Centralized borrowing operations have one department that accepts requests, initiates and maintains online transactions, notifies patrons, and distributes materials. Centralized borrowing units handle requests from all types of individuals. Centralized lending operations bring together request receipt, call number lookup, stack retrieval, photocopying, charging/discharging, maintenance of online transactions, and possibly wrapping and unwrapping, regardless of the material's location.

Typically, decentralized borrowing signifies that branch and/or departmental libraries handle the complete process for their primary clientele. Decentralized lending usually indicates that staff in branch and/or departmental libraries handle all steps of the lending process, from receiving new lending requests, retrieving material, and photocopying to wrapping and/or sending materials.

Table 26 compares the average performance of decentralized operations with the average performance of centralized operations in research libraries, and with ILL operations in all 97 research libraries. A similar comparison for college libraries was not possible as there was only one college library with a decentralized ILL operation. Because participants were assured confidentiality of institution-specific data, it is not possible to present data for that single college library participant. **Table 26 suggests that decentralized borrowing results in a lower unit cost, faster turnaround time, and a slightly higher fill rate. However, economies of scale are more evident with centralized lending because centralization results in lower unit costs and higher fill rates than the average for all 97 research libraries.**

In participating research libraries, ILL is most often part of the Public Services Department or the Access Services Department, whereas ILL departments in college libraries are either part of the Reference Department or the Public Services Department. Only three research libraries and two college libraries include the ILL unit as part of the Acquisitions or Technical Services departments.

For both groups of libraries, just over half of the ILL operations are managed by an administrative head, defined by the Study as an individual assigned policy-making and planning responsibility. The administrative head may be a department head or a librarian with supervisory responsibilities. Another 40% of the ILL departments are managed by a support staff supervisor, defined by the Study as full-time library staff in a clerical, para-professional, or support staff position with supervisory responsibility.

Nearly sixty percent (59%) of research libraries and 45% of college libraries have separate budgets for borrowing expenses. It is worth repeating Graham Cornish's admonition in his 1991 report of a European survey of interlending and document supply:

> It is disturbing that so few libraries view interlending as important enough to warrant a separate budget. Of course, there is the other side of the argument, namely that by 'hiding' the costs of interlending in some other activity it can be expanded at the expense of something else without attracting the notice of administrators. In the long run, however, this is not the way to establish the worth and importance of this activity.[19]

[19] Graham P. Cornish, "A European-Wide Survey of Interlending and Document Supply," *Interlending and Document Supply* 19 (April 1991): 51.

3.6.5 Staffing

In half of the participating research libraries, staff work a 40-hour week, with the others evenly split between a 35- and a 37.5-hour workweek. Staff in participating college libraries are evenly divided among a 35-, 37.5-, and a 40-hour workweek.

Only one of the 22 college libraries report a unionized support staff, and just four have professional staff with faculty status. The level of unionization in research libraries is quite different: 17 research libraries have unionized professional staff and 46 have unionized support staff. Professional staff in 39 research libraries have faculty status.

3.6.6 Borrowing Policies

Two-thirds of research and college library participants do not limit the number of requests local patrons may submit at one time. Although both groups of libraries permit patrons to submit ILL requests at multiple service points, the ILL office is the most common location. Two-thirds of all participants offer patrons an electronic ordering capability.

Patrons in nearly three-quarters (72%) of the research libraries retrieve materials at the ILL office, whereas the most common pick-up point in college libraries is the circulation desk (82%). Although both groups of libraries offer multiple pick-up points, only two research libraries and one college library mail books directly to patrons. For photocopies, 71% of the research libraries and 91% of the college libraries send photocopies to patrons via campus mail or the postal service.

A total of 61% of research libraries and 71% of college libraries establish reciprocal agreements with other libraries to avoid processing and/or paying lending fees. The amount spent to borrow a book or obtain a photocopy reflects their preference for reciprocal agreements. On average, research libraries spend $2.65 and college libraries spend $1.85 per transaction on borrowing fees. Borrowing fees include library lending or photocopy charges, document delivery supplier fees, payments to the Copyright Clearance Center, etc.

3.6.7 Lending Charging and Payment Policies

Ninety-two percent (92%) of the 97 research libraries and 64% of the 22 college libraries charge to lend books or supply photocopies. Fees to supply photocopies are more common than fees to lend books (89% to 70% for the 89 research libraries; 64% to 55% for the 22 college libraries).

Checks are the most commonly accepted payment method (82% of research libraries and 68% of college libraries). Only 15 research libraries and no college library accept credit cards for payment. Income received from lending operations is retained by 44% of the ILL departments in research libraries and 32% of the ILL departments in college libraries.

3.6.8 Use of Document Delivery Suppliers

A total of 93 of the 97 research library participants borrow for local users. For these 93, 86 (92%) use document delivery suppliers. For this group, suppliers fill, on average, 12% of all photocopy requests. Nineteen (19) of the 22 college library participants use document delivery suppliers, which fill, on average, 15% of their photocopy requests.

The Study explored the borrowing performance of the 19 research libraries that used document delivery suppliers to fill 20% or more of their photocopy requests. For this subgroup, mean turnaround time for non-returnables was 13.8 calendar days, 8% faster than average turnaround time for all 97 research library participants. The mean borrowing unit cost was $19.61, 7% more than the average $18.35 borrowing unit cost for all research libraries. **For this subset of 19 research libraries, there is no correlation between unit cost and use of document suppliers and no correlation between fill rate and use of document suppliers. In spite of having slightly faster average turnaround time than all 97 research library participants, the slightly positive correlation between turnaround time and use of document suppliers for this subset suggests that as their use of document suppliers increases, turnaround time also increases, rather than decreases, as most librarians assume.** Many libraries use document suppliers because they believe they will receive materials faster than if they use libraries. **However, additional research is needed to explore why turnaround time does not decrease as use of document delivery suppliers increases.**

The Study did not ask participants to indicate why they chose document delivery suppliers instead of libraries. However, the modest use of document suppliers gives weight to reports from other studies about the ILL managers' preference to rely on reciprocal agreements to avoid paying fees, the low fill rate of document suppliers for the kind of material requested by research or college library patrons, the slow turnaround time from document suppliers compared to preferred lending libraries, or the lack of funds to pay document delivery supplier charges.[20]

This Study did not undertake to compare lending/supply performance of libraries and document suppliers. A number of institution-specific studies of turnaround time, fill rate, and charges (not costs) have been reported in the library literature, but none is on a scale comparable to this Study.[21] It is unlikely that document suppliers will be willing to reveal their direct per transaction costs, but it is reasonable to assume that their charges and fees cover most, if not all, of their direct costs. **The comparison of lending performance between libraries and document suppliers is an area worthy of additional research.**

3.6.9   Level of Difficulty of Requests

The General Characteristics Questionnaire asked participants to record the level of difficulty of verifying borrowing and lending requests. For borrowing, verification is the process of confirming accuracy of the citation and finding potential lenders/suppliers. The verification process for lending involves determining whether the item is owned, recording the call number, and noting which libraries within the institution own the item. Recognizing that all libraries receive requests of varying degrees of difficulty during the course of a year, the question sought a subjective, generalized response.

Half (50%) of the research library and 59% of college library respondents characterized the level of verification difficulty of their borrowing requests (requests from their local patrons) as *average*. Only two of the 22 Oberlin Group libraries characterized their borrowing requests as *fairly difficult* to verify, whereas 18 research libraries indicated that their borrowing requests were *fairly difficult*. None of the 119 participants indicated that their borrowing requests were *very difficult* to verify. At the other extreme, 26 research libraries and seven college libraries considered their borrowing requests *very easy* or *fairly easy* to verify.

Lending requests, on average, were easier to verify than borrowing requests for both groups. Just under

half (45%) of research libraries characterized the verification difficulty of lending requests as *average*, with an additional 50% of research libraries indicating *fairly easy* or *very easy*. College libraries were almost evenly split, with 41% characterizing the verification difficulty as *average* and 36% as *fairly easy*. Only five research libraries and no college libraries considered their lending requests *fairly difficult* or *very difficult* to verify.

3.6.10   International ILL/DD

Virtually all (95%) of the 119 participants engage in international ILL, either as a borrower, a lender/supplier, or both. The ranking of areas/countries most frequently cited either as a borrower or lender reflects the degree to which potential lenders can be identified and the relative concern about materials being lost in shipment or return. U.S. libraries ranked Canadian libraries as their most common international trading partners, and the reverse was true for Canadian libraries. Use of libraries in other parts of the world was much less common, with European libraries the next most likely trading partners for both Canadian and U.S. libraries, for both borrowing and lending.

3.6.11   Electronic Request Transmission Methods

Most libraries transmit and receive ILL requests by one or more electronic messaging systems. In the United States, OCLC, RLIN, WLN, and DOCLINE dominate. In Canada, ENVOY and other email-based systems reflect the Canadian preference for point-to-point communication. Table 27 summarizes the use of four ILL messaging systems by U.S. research and some Canadian research libraries. This table excludes use of all other automated and non-automated requesting methods, and because none of the college library participants uses RLIN, WLN, or DOCLINE, this table also excludes college libraries.

3.6.12   OCLC ILL-Related Features

Because of the extensive use of the OCLC ILL system, the General Characteristics Questionnaire asked participants about their use of a variety of OCLC ILL-related

---

[20] See Footnote 13 for selected articles.
[21] See Footnote 13 for selected articles.

TABLE 27	Use of Bibliographic Utilities' ILL Systems: Research Libraries			
	Borrowing		Lending	
	# libraries using	% of participants	# libraries using	% of participants
OCLC only	50	60%	54	60%
OCLC, RLIN	18	22%	20	22%
OCLC, DOCLINE	12	15%	11	13%
OCLC, RLIN, DOCLINE	1	1%	2	2%
OCLC, WLN, DOCLINE	1	1%	1	1%
DOCLINE only	1	1%	2	2%
Total	83	100%	90	100%

features. The level of use of these features is shown in Figure 5.

Virtually all OCLC ILL-related features are designed to reduce staff involvement at various steps of the transaction. Each feature is summarized below. Several findings are noteworthy. College library participants make more extensive use of all of the OCLC ILL-related features with the exception of ILL Prism Transfer (IPT), which enables patron email requests to be transferred into the OCLC ILL Review File.

CHECKING UNION LISTS enables borrowers to verify detailed serial holdings of potential lenders, increasing fill rates for both borrowers and lenders.

THE ILL MICROENHANCER (ILLME) is OCLC workstation software that permits batch (off-line) updating of ILL transactions, saving staff time, and permitting use of equipment when staff are not working.

THE ILL FEE MANAGEMENT (IFM) is a service in which lending fees and borrowing payments are posted to the library's monthly OCLC statement, eliminating staff handling of per-transaction invoices and payments.

CUSTOM HOLDINGS PATHS are strings of preferred lenders set up by the borrowing library to reduce the need to look at multiple screens of symbols of potential lenders in order to select a specific group of preferred lenders.

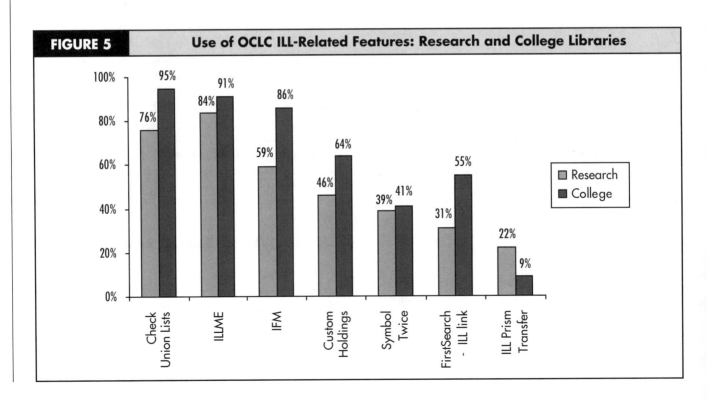

FIGURE 5 — Use of OCLC ILL-Related Features: Research and College Libraries

"ENTER MY SYMBOL TWICE" is a feature that lending libraries may activate. It requires borrowing libraries to enter a lending library's symbol two times, thus giving that lender eight days, rather than the standard four days, to respond. This may be the only feature that does not directly reduce staff involvement.

THE FIRST SEARCH-TO-PRISM ILL TRANSFER enables patrons to transfer journal article citations found in FirstSearch citation databases to the ILL Review File for processing by their local ILL departments, eliminating the need for staff to re-search and re-key bibliographic information.

ILL PRISM TRANSFER (IPT) moves patron email requests into the ILL Review File of the patron's local library, again eliminating the need for staff to re-search and re-key bibliographic information.

Although use of any of these features is not statistically significant, it is likely that one of the contributing factors to the college libraries' higher fill rates and lower unit costs is their more extensive use of the various OCLC ILL-related features, particularly their use of custom holdings and the activation of the FirstSearch-ILL link.

3.6.13 Management Software

Many research library respondents use some form of software to manage ILL transactions. In research libraries, 40 borrowing operations use SAVEIT and nine use AVISO. For lending, 30 libraries use SAVEIT and seven use AVISO. SAVEIT, a software program developed by Patrick Brumbaugh at Case Western University, is now available from his company, Interlibrary Software and Services, Inc. AVISO, a management software product originally developed by Dave Binkley, a Canadian ILL librarian, is now owned and marketed by A-G Canada, Ltd. QuickDOC (a similar software product for medical libraries developed and marketed by Jay Daly), PRS (developed by ILL staff at Brigham Young University Libraries), EXCEL (commercial software), or locally-developed software are used by eight borrowing operations and seven lending operations.[22]

Use of management software in college libraries is less common. Nine college libraries use SAVEIT for borrowing and seven for lending. No college library uses AVISO or any other commercial or locally-developed management software.

3.6.14 Equipment

Just over half (55%) of research library participants and 73% of college library participants provide one workstation per FTE staff. A workstation was defined as a computer able to access the local online catalog, national bibliographic utilities, Internet resources, and/or local management software.

Participants were asked to list equipment located in the ILL office and equipment housed in other parts of the library but accessed by ILL staff. Online public access terminals (terminals or workstations to access local online catalogs) are installed in 76% of the ILL departments in research libraries and 73% of the ILL departments in college libraries. Fax machines are located in 77% of research libraries' ILL departments and 45% of college libraries' ILL departments. Only 18% of the college libraries' ILL departments have a photocopy machine in their office, while 82% of research libraries' ILL departments are equipped with a photocopy machine.

3.6.15 Delivery Preferences

Virtually all 119 participants indicated that postal service and fax are the most frequently used delivery methods for borrowing or lending. Between one-half and three-quarters of all participants also use state/regional couriers and/or surface delivery services (FedEx, Pony Express, UPS, etc.).

Research libraries' use of Ariel, document delivery software developed by the Research Libraries Group for Internet users, varies between borrowing and lending. A total of 75 research libraries (81% of participants that borrow) use Ariel to receive articles, and 84 libraries (87% of participants that lend) use Ariel to transmit articles. Use of Ariel by college library participants is not quite as extensive. Half (50%) of the college libraries use Ariel as a borrower and a lender, but two college libraries use Ariel to send articles, not to receive articles. The Study did not ask why participants use Ariel for just one operation.

3.7 FINAL OBSERVATIONS

This section highlights some general characteristics of the ILL operations of the 119 North American research

---

[22] At the time the questionnaire was distributed, the CLIO management software had not been introduced to the library market. CLIO, distributed by Perkins and Associates, is Windows-based software with much the same functionality as the other products mentioned in this section.

and college library participants. Most ILL departments have centralized borrowing and lending operations that are administratively part of public services departments. Support staff supervisors are slightly favored over professional supervisors to manage ILL operations.

Virtually all operations use some form of electronic communication to send and receive requests, and many use electronic delivery technologies to send and receive materials. Just less than half of all 119 participants use some type of software to manage internal files.

Findings from many questions on the General Characteristics Questionnaire were correlated with cost, turnaround time, and fill rate; no significant positive or negative correlations were found. The characteristics of ILL operations in research and college libraries summarized in this section may not directly change any of the performance measures, but the overview provides a glimpse into how current ILL operations in North American research and college libraries are organized and managed.

4 ILL/DD OPERATIONS IN OHIOLINK LIBRARIES

The cost advantages of shifting traffic to user-initiated systems, to the extent those systems are able to fill requests, are attractive.

The variation in borrowing unit costs among four Ohio-LINK participants clearly reflects the effect of different transaction levels. Unit costs for the two libraries that included p-circ transactions in their transaction totals (Cincinnati and Ohio University) are significantly lower than the two that excluded p-circ transactions (Kent State and Ohio State).

User-initiated interlibrary loan, as exemplified by the OhioLINK and ILLINET Online systems, has emerged as an attractive alternative to traditional, staff-mediated interlibrary loan. The experience of these services suggests that the unit cost of filling one request through an unmediated circulation-like transaction is less than the unit cost of filling that same request through the traditional, mediated interlibrary loan process. In order to test the belief that user-initiated ILL is a cost-effective alternative, the Study examined in detail findings of four research institutions that use OhioLINK for ILL: University of Cincinnati,[23] Kent State University, Ohio State University, and Ohio University.

These four libraries are active participants in Ohio-LINK, a centralized union catalog representing, in 1998, collections of more than 56 Ohio public and private academic libraries plus the State Library of Ohio. OhioLINK's catalog permits a user to locate which libraries own the needed title, but, even more importantly, to initiate a direct (unmediated) request to have the item sent to the patron's local library. A software algorithm, not the user, selects the potential lender based on ownership and availability. Circulation or ILL staff in the owning library retrieve the item and send it via a statewide ground courier service to the patron's library. Upon receipt, the patron's library generates a material available notice. OhioLINK participants refer to this process as a "p-circ" transaction.[24]

Because this process occurs between libraries not administratively linked and because transactions are handled by ILL staff, some participants consider these interlibrary loan transactions. Others view p-circ transactions as an enhanced form of circulation and include them in their circulation statistics, in part because requests are handled by circulation staff. Because of these differing views, there is no consistency in counting and reporting these transactions. These differing views of how to count and report user-initiated requests are not unique to OhioLINK member libraries but are shared by other libraries that have activated patron-initiated ordering capabilities.

This section summarizes the findings of the main ILL operations of the University of Cincinnati, Kent State University, Ohio State University, and Ohio University. Turnaround time, fill rate, and user satisfaction are

summarized, followed by a detailed examination of unit costs. Directors and staff in these libraries were interested in comparing ILL performance among themselves, but found this was not possible because Cincinnati and Ohio University included p-circ transactions in their ILL borrowing and lending totals reported for this Study, while Kent State and Ohio State did not. Directors of the four OhioLINK research libraries gave written permission for their institution-specific data to be disclosed in an analysis and for the results to be published. A series of tables presents the four participants' unit costs and demonstrates the impact on unit costs of including or excluding user-initiated transactions with mediated interlibrary loan transactions. This analysis is included to illustrate some of the challenges that exist in finding comparative measures of mediated and unmediated ILL and to showcase a promising approach to effective ILL services.

4.1 TURNAROUND TIME, FILL RATE, AND USER SATISFACTION FOR OHIOLINK PARTICIPANTS

The performance of the ILL operations in the four OhioLINK libraries is comparable to the average performance of all research libraries. The following findings include p-circ and mediated interlibrary loan transactions; it was not possible to disaggregate turnaround time, fill rate, and user satisfaction levels for p-circ and mediated ILL transactions.

As borrowers, the four libraries have a slightly lower fill rate, 80%, than the 85% average of all research libraries. However, the lending fill rate of 63%, 5% higher than the 58% average of all research libraries, suggests that lenders receive requests known to be available in their libraries. It is unclear why knowledge of holdings and availability did not increase the borrowing fill rate.

Average turnaround time for all requests is 12.6 calendar days, nearly 25% faster than the average turnaround time for all research libraries. P-circ materials, which account for 74% of total borrowing volume reported by the four research libraries, are delivered via a statewide courier, funded centrally by OhioLINK, within

---

[23] The University of Cincinnati was represented by two ILL operations: the main library and the Health Sciences Library. Because of the different character of medical library ILL operations, the following analysis excludes Cincinnati's Health Sciences Library and focuses on the main ILL operations of the four research libraries.

[24] At present OhioLINK does not handle photocopy transactions; thus, a user-initiated transaction is equivalent to and reported in the following statistics as a returnable transaction. For these libraries, p-circ transactions represent 74% of the total returnables reported for borrowing, and 63% of the total returnables reported for lending.

24 hours of shipment. For p-circ and mediated-ILL returnables, the four OhioLINK participants averaged 15.0 calendar days, nearly two days faster than the average for all 97 research library participants. For non-returnables (all handled as mediated ILL transactions), average turnaround time was 14.4 calendar days, only half a day faster than all research libraries.

As with other research libraries, users at the four Ohio-LINK libraries were very satisfied with the overall service. Users at the four OhioLINK libraries were slightly less satisfied with the timeliness of delivery (90%) than users at all research libraries (94%). Satisfaction with the quality of material received, 98%, was one percentage point higher than all research libraries, and satisfaction with staff was the same as all research libraries (95%).

TABLE 28

Borrowing and Lending Volume: OhioLINK Participants

	Borrowing Volume	Lending Volume
Cincinnati	39,057	36,101
Kent State	9,072	14,992
Ohio State	11,757	19,688
Ohio U.	30,514	42,483

4.2   VOLUME OF TRANSACTIONS REPORTED BY OHIOLINK PARTICIPANTS

Table 28 presents the annual volume of ILL transactions as reported by the four OhioLINK participants. Cincinnati and Ohio University, which included p-circ transactions, reported three to four times the borrowing

volume and two to three times the lending volume of Kent State and Ohio State, which did not include p-circ transactions in their totals.

4.3   P-CIRC AND ILL TRANSACTION VOLUMES DISAGGREGATED

In order to explore the effect of p-circ transactions on unit cost, the four participants were asked to provide separate totals for p-circ and ILL transactions. Ohio State also supplied a copy of OhioLINK's FY96 statistical report. Unfortunately, the totals on the OhioLINK report varied from the p-circ transactions reported by the four libraries. To ensure consistency with data reported for the Study, the p-circ totals (or estimates) were used rather than data from the OhioLINK statistical report. Table 29 summarizes p-circ and ILL totals as reported by each participant.

4.4   UNIT COSTS RECALCULATED WITH DISAGGREGATED TRANSACTION VOLUMES

Total expenditures for the four OhioLINK participants were calculated by multiplying the unit cost by the transaction volume they reported for the Study. **However, totals reported for the Study do not reflect total expenditures for all p-circ and ILL transactions.** Ohio State did not report any costs for handling p-circ transactions because p-circ transactions are handled by circulation staff. Similarly, Kent State did not report any costs associated with p-circ borrowing requests because at the time of the Study those requests were handled by circulation staff. None of the four participants reported delivery costs for any p-circ transactions because OhioLINK centrally funds a statewide courier service. Therefore, the total ILL/DD expenditures shown in Table 30 underrepresent total expenditures for p-circ and ILL transactions.

TABLE 29	P-circ and ILL Transactions Disaggregated: OhioLINK Participants					
	Borrowing			Lending		
	P-circ	ILL	Total	P-circ	ILL	Total
Cincinnati	29,708	9,349	39,057	25,121	10,980	36,101
Kent State	24,363	9,072	33,435	15,761	14,992	30,753
Ohio State	38,000	11,757	49,757	47,000	19,688	66,688
Ohio U.	22,490	8,024	30,514	26,805	15,678	42,483

TABLE 30		
Total ILL/DD Expenditures: OhioLINK Participants		
	Borrowing	Lending
Cincinnati	$234,342	$140,072
Kent State	$177,811	$136,127
Ohio State	$182,469	$142,344
Ohio U.	$154,401	$140,619

Remembering that total expenditures shown in Table 30 do not include all costs associated with handling p-circ *and* interlibrary loan transactions, it is possible only to estimate unit costs for p-circ, ILL, and total transactions. Unit costs presented in Table 31 were calculated by dividing total expenditures (Table 30) by p-circ volume, ILL volume, and total volume (Table 29). The estimated unit costs reported in Table 31 corroborate how volume of transactions affects unit cost.

4.5 FINAL OBSERVATIONS

OhioLINK provides low cost, user-initiated ILL that is envied by many. However, because patron-initiated circulation transactions are handled by ILL staff in some libraries and by circulation staff in other libraries, it is misleading to compare the unit costs of the four OhioLINK libraries without understanding the factors that contribute to those unit costs.

The purpose of this comparison was to show that there are different costs associated with operating user-initiated and staff-mediated services. The cost advantages of shifting traffic to user-initiated systems, to the extent those systems are able to fill requests, are attractive. However, this section only estimated costs associated with user-initiated requesting by OhioLINK libraries. **Additional research on the cost and performance of OhioLINK user-initiated transactions is highly desirable. Such a study could use the methodology employed in this investigation to collect data on the cost and performance of p-circ transactions, regardless of where those transactions are processed. The same study could examine the portion of unit cost paid by the participating libraries and by OhioLINK central funding, and compare the differences in performance between p-circ and mediated interlibrary loan in a larger sample of OhioLINK libraries.**

TABLE 31	Estimated Mean Borrowing and Lending Unit Costs for P-circ, ILL, and Combined Transactions: OhioLINK Participants					
	Borrowing			Lending		
	P-circ	ILL	Total	P-circ	ILL	Total
Cincinnati	$7.89	$25.07	$6.00	$5.58	$12.76	$3.88
Kent State	$7.30	$19.60	$5.32	$8.64	$9.08	$4.43
Ohio State	$0.31	$15.52	$3.67	$3.03	$7.23	$2.13
Ohio U.	$6.87	$19.24	$5.06	$5.25	$8.97	$3.31

5 ILL/DD OPERATIONS IN CANADIAN RESEARCH LIBRARIES

When ILL operations in Canadian and U.S. university libraries are compared and even when transaction volume is held constant, the mean borrowing unit cost for the 11 Canadian university libraries is $3.00 more than the mean unit cost for the U.S. university libraries. A regression analysis found that the difference is not statistically significant, but the Study could not identify any causes for the difference.

5.1   SUMMARY OF THE PERFORMANCE MEASURES

Thirteen Canadian research libraries participated in the Study: nine main libraries and four branch or departmental libraries. Eleven represented university libraries, and two were government research libraries. ILL operations in Canadian and U.S. libraries vary in a number of ways, including access to holdings, methods of request transmission, use of technology, and the central lending/supply role of several major university and national libraries. This section summarizes the

performance of interlibrary loan operations for the 13 Canadian participants, and, where appropriate, compares their performance with the 84 U.S. research libraries and/or the 22 U.S. college libraries. Means and medians were calculated with data from all 13 Canadian participants, but, like other tables in this report, the ranges reflect the middle 80% of Canadian participants. That is, data on libraries in the highest (90 - 100th percentile) and lowest (0 - 10th percentile) performance ranges are excluded from all figures and tables in this section. Finally, because of the small number of Canadian participants, no regional breakdown is included in order to assure confidentiality of

TABLE 32	1996 Performance of ILL/DD Operations in Canadian Research Libraries			
	10th percentile	Mean	Median	90th percentile
Total Transactions	8,797	51,453	22,605	99,102
Borrowing	1,209	7,991	7,319	13,881
Returnables	280	2,848	2,813	5,816
Non-returnables	803	5,143	2,714	23,692
Lending	5,021	43,463	14,725	69,732
Returnables	1,033	8,281	7,358	17,652
Non-returnables	2,488	35,266	10,533	52,080
Unit Cost[25]				
Borrowing	$15.90	$28.81	$19.86	$54.98
Lending	$ 6.26	$ 9.95	$ 8.61	$14.69
Fill Rate				
Borrowing	76%	83%	85%	98%
Lending	62%	77%	79%	94%
Turnaround Time				
Total	12.8 days	17.5 days	16.2 days	23.6 days
Returnables	16.2 days	20.5 days	19.7 days	26.8 days
Non-returnables	10.8 days	16.2 days	13.8 days	21.9 days
User Satisfaction				
Timeliness	88%	93%	95%	96%
Quality	95%	98%	97%	100%
Staff	84%	97%	99%	100%
User Paid	0%	32%	30%	64%
Amount Paid	$0.00	$6.59	$4.14	$7.35
Willing to Pay	$1.47	$2.99	$2.34	$5.82

[25] All dollar amounts are expressed in U.S. currency. Canadian participants submitted data in Canadian currency; the Study converted Canadian dollars to U. S. dollars using 1.3613 Canadian dollars to one U.S. dollar, the conversion figure used in *ARL Statistics 1995-96*. See Appendix D for Tables 32, 33, and 34 expressed in Canadian currency.

individual institutions. Table 32 summarizes the performance of the 13 Canadian participants.

As noted in Table 32, the performance of ILL operations in Canadian research libraries varies. The mean borrowing unit cost for the 13 Canadian participants is $28.81, 73% higher than the $16.67 mean unit cost for the 84 U.S. research libraries. The mean lending unit cost is $9.95, 6% higher than the $9.39 mean lending unit cost for U.S. research libraries.

The average borrowing fill rate is 83%, with a range from 76% to 98%. The average borrowing fill rate for the 84 U.S. research libraries is a comparable 85%. Canadian libraries fill 77% of their lending requests, compared with a mean lending fill rate of 55% for all U.S. libraries, one area in which Canadian libraries significantly outperform their U.S. counterparts.

Borrowing turnaround time averages 17.5 calendar days for all requests, 2.4 days longer than U.S. research libraries. Canadian libraries take, on average, 20.5 calendar days to complete a borrowing transaction for a returnable, and 16.2 days for a non-returnable, both slower than the average for all U.S. research libraries (16.3 and 14.5 respectively). As Table 33 indicates, Canadian libraries obtain 28% of all requests within seven calendar days, identical to the 28% for the 84 U.S. research libraries. For returnables, Canadian participants obtain 18% within seven calendar days, less than the 24% for U.S. research libraries. For non-returnables, Canadian participants receive 35% within seven calendar days, slightly higher than the 30% average for all 84 U.S. research libraries.

Users of ILL/DD operations in Canadian libraries are almost equally satisfied with the timeliness of the request (93% to 94% for the 84 U.S. research libraries), the quality of the request (98% to 97%), and their interaction with staff (97% to 94%). More users pay for requests, 32% compared with 5% for their U.S. counterparts, although the average amount paid is slightly less—$6.59 to $6.89. Canadian patrons are willing to

pay $2.99, somewhat more than the $2.64 average for the 84 U.S. research libraries.

5.2 VOLUME OF BORROWING AND LENDING & PROPORTION OF RETURNABLES TO NON-RETURNABLES

As detailed in Table 32, the average borrowing and lending requests (7,991 and 43,463, respectively) filled by Canadian libraries vary from the average of the 84 U.S. research libraries (14,293 and 25,232, respectively). On average, Canadian libraries handle 44% fewer borrowing requests and 42% more lending requests than their U.S. counterparts. For Canadian participants, lending requests average 84% of their total ILL activity; however the median for the 13 Canadian participants is 65%, comparable to the average of the 84 U.S. research libraries.

For borrowing, Canadian libraries obtain more non-returnables (64%) than do U.S. research libraries (48%). Lending operations in Canadian research libraries supply a significantly higher percentage of non-returnables (81%) than the 84 U.S. research libraries (59%).

5.3 UNIT COSTS

The breakdown of unit cost by cost category for Canadian participants varies from the average of the 84 U.S. research libraries. Table 34 summarizes Canadian borrowing and lending unit costs by cost category.

Given the central, but unique, roles played by CISTI and the National Library of Canada, data from just Canadian and U.S. research universities were examined. **When ILL operations in Canadian and U.S. university libraries are compared and even when transaction volume is held constant, the mean borrowing unit cost in Canadian university libraries is $3.00 more**

TABLE 33	Cumulative Mean Borrowing Turnaround Time: Canadian Libraries		
	All Requests	Returnables	Non-returnables
0-3 calendar days	4%	2%	6%
0-7 calendar days	28%	18%	35%
0-14 calendar days	58%	55%	69%
0-21 calendar days	78%	76%	81%

than the mean unit cost in U.S. university libraries. A regression analysis found that the difference is not statistically significant, but the Study could not identify any causes for the difference. The Study ruled out a number of possible causes, but this also remains an area for additional study.

Another way to examine mean unit costs of the 13 Canadian participants is to compare them with the 84 U.S. research library participants and the 22 college library participants. Table 35 shows those differences.

The breakdown of unit cost by cost category for the Canadian participants differs from the 84 U.S. research libraries and the 22 college library participants. Table 36 compares percentage of borrowing unit cost spent on each cost category and Table 37 presents the same comparison for lending.

5.4 ORGANIZATION AND ADMINISTRATION

On average, Canadian libraries have 2.9 ILL processing units, slightly higher than the average of 2.5 reported for the 84 U.S. research libraries. However, the number of branch or departmental libraries served by the central ILL operation (4) is half of the number served by U.S. research libraries (8). All borrowing operations in Canadian research library participants are centralized, and 12 of the 13 have centralized lending operations.

TABLE 34 — Mean Borrowing and Lending Unit Costs by Cost Category: Canadian Participants	Borrowing	Lending
Staff	$19.37	$8.19
ILL Staff	$18.19	$6.38
Staff in other depts.	$ 1.18	$1.81
Network/communication	$ 2.16	$0.25
Delivery	$ 0.62	$0.66
Photocopying	$ 0.07	$0.22
Supplies	$ 0.19	$0.19
Equipment	$ 1.58	$0.44
Borrowing fees	$ 4.82	n/a
Total	$28.81	$9.95

TABLE 35 — Comparison of Mean Borrowing and Lending Unit Costs: Canadian, U.S. Research, and College Libraries	13 Canadian Libraries	84 U.S. Research Libraries	22 College Libraries
Borrowing	$28.81	$16.67	$12.08
Lending	$ 9.95	$ 9.39	$ 7.25

TABLE 36 — Comparison of Mean Borrowing Unit Costs by Cost Category: Canadian, U.S. Research, and College Libraries	13 Canadian Libraries	84 U.S. Research Libraries	22 College Libraries
Staff	67%	64%	62%
Network/communication	8%	14%	13%
Delivery	2%	4%	6%
Photocopy	0%	0%	0%
Supplies	1%	1%	1%
Equipment	5%	3%	3%
Borrowing fees	17%	14%	15%
Total	100%	100%	100%

TABLE 37	Comparison of Mean Lending Unit Costs by Cost Category: Canadian, U.S. Research, and College Libraries		
	13 Canadian Libraries	84 U.S. Research Libraries	22 College Libraries
Staff	82%	75%	71%
Network/communication	3%	4%	6%
Delivery	7%	11%	14%
Photocopy	2%	5%	3%
Supplies	2%	2%	2%
Equipment	4%	3%	4%
Total	100%	100%	100%

5.5   STAFFING

The proportion of all staff with ILL responsibilities who work in ILL departments (94%) is slightly higher than all U.S. research libraries ILL department staff (86%). This difference suggests a slightly more centralized approach to borrowing and lending in the 13 Canadian libraries. **However, it is the mix of staff positions used in Canadian research libraries that varies significantly from U.S. research or college libraries.** Table 38 displays the type and proportion of staff processing borrowing requests and Table 39 compares lending staff. These tables combine staff working in the ILL department with staff with ILL responsibilities working in other departments within the library.

TABLE 38	Comparison of Mean Borrowing Staff by Staff Category: Canadian, U.S. Research, and College Libraries		
	13 Canadian Libraries	84 U.S. Research Libraries	22 College Libraries
Professional supervisor	15%	17%	28%
Professional non-supervisor	3%	9%	11%
Support staff supervisor	11%	20%	24%
Support staff	70%	45%	28%
Students	1%	9%	9%
Total	100%	100%	100%

TABLE 39	Comparison of Mean Lending Staff by Staff Category: Canadian, U.S. Research, and College Libraries		
	13 Canadian Libraries	84 U.S. Research Libraries	22 College Libraries
Professional supervisor	12%	11%	19%
Professional non-supervisor	1%	4%	2%
Support staff supervisor	13%	14%	17%
Support staff	72%	55%	38%
Students	2%	16%	24%
Total	100%	100%	100%

5.6 BORROWING POLICIES

Like U.S. research and college libraries, Canadian libraries have established a variety of reciprocal agreements to facilitate ILL. Regional consortial reciprocal agreements were the most commonly reported; seven borrowing operations and seven lending operations have established such agreements. The next most common type of reciprocal agreement is with individual libraries, with nine of the 13 libraries having established agreements with one or more libraries for borrowing and lending. Canadian libraries, however, rely somewhat less on reciprocal agreements than the 84 U.S. research library participants do. Just less than half (48%) of the borrowing requests generated by the 13 Canadian participants are filled by libraries using reciprocal agreements in order to avoid processing and/or payment of lending fees, compared with 70% for their U.S. counterparts.

Seven ILL units offer electronic forms for patrons to submit requests. Twelve of the 13 do not limit the number of requests patrons can submit at any one time. Nine do not charge patrons for loan requests, but nine libraries do charge their patrons for photocopy requests. The ILL office is the most common pick-up point for both returnables and non-returnables. **Unlike most U.S. research and college libraries, Canadian libraries do not mail photocopies directly to patrons but require them to pick up articles at their local ILL offices.**

5.7 LENDING CHARGING AND PAYMENT POLICIES

Ten of the 13 Canadian research libraries charge other libraries to fill loan requests and 12 charge the borrower to supply photocopies. Six of the 13 ILL units keep the lending income received. Comparable to U.S. research and college libraries, checks are the most commonly accepted payment method, and only four accept credit cards as a payment method.

5.8 USE OF DOCUMENT DELIVERY SUPPLIERS

Twelve of the 13 Canadian participants (92%) use document suppliers, somewhat more than the aggregate of the 84 U.S. research libraries (88%). Document suppliers filled 20% of their photocopy requests, compared with 11% for the U.S. research libraries. It is likely that Canadian participants record document suppliers as filling a larger percentage of photocopy requests because they choose to send requests to CISTI, which many consider to be a document supplier. Because the Study did not ask participants to provide supplier-specific data, it is impossible to confirm that speculation.

5.9 INTERNATIONAL ILL/DD

All Canadian participants engage in international interlibrary loan, either as a borrower, a lender, or both. Canadian libraries turn to U.S. libraries as their most common international trading partners, followed by European libraries. Only two libraries estimated the volume of international ILL, so it is not possible to ascertain the percentage of international borrowing or lending for Canadian libraries.

5.10 EQUIPMENT AND MANAGEMENT SOFTWARE

Seven libraries use AVISO to manage their borrowing requests and five use AVISO to manage their lending requests. AVISO is a software product developed by a Canadian ILL librarian and now owned and marketed by A-G Canada, Ltd. AVISO is similar to SAVEIT and CLIO software, but also includes a messaging component, one of the features that makes AVISO preferable to other management software packages for Canadians. Use of Ariel for borrowing and lending is very high—all use Ariel to send requests, and all but one use Ariel to receive articles.

The variety of ILL department equipment and software is comparable to all U.S. research libraries—most have fax machines, online public access terminals, and multiple access workstations. Six of the 13 (46%) Canadian participants provide one workstation per FTE, somewhat less than their U.S. counterparts (56%).

5.11 ELECTRONIC REQUEST TRANSMISSION METHODS

One area in which Canadian libraries differ significantly from their U.S. counterparts is how they communicate with other libraries. Canadian ILL operations favor point-to-point email communication, in part because of the National Library of Canada's leading role in the development of the international standard for ILL communication (ISO ILL Protocol 10160 & 10161). Table 40 summarizes the methods by which Canadian libraries send and receive ILL requests, the

TABLE 40	Use of Various Transmission Methods: Canadian Participants			
	Borrowing		Lending	
	Number of Libraries	Average % of Requests Sent via	Number of Libraries	Average % of Requests Received via
Email/Internet	11	50%	11	43%
Mail/post	11	6%	11	11%
Fax	10	18%	9	7%
Other*	8	25%	11	32%
OCLC	5	24%	7	5%
Ariel	2	5%	7	4%
DOCLINE	3	13%	3	40%
Supplier dedicated system	3	28%	0	
RLIN	0		0	
WLN	0		0	
OPAC ILL module	0		2	43%

* Participants did not give examples, but this category may include requests made by phone, delivered by messengers, etc.

number of libraries using each method, and the average percentage of requests sent or received. **This table clearly illustrates the Canadian preference for email communication.**

5.12 FINAL OBSERVATIONS

ILL/DD operations in Canadian research libraries provide a level of service comparable with that provided by U.S. research libraries. Three differences are noteworthy. First, Canadian libraries, on average, process fewer borrowing and lending transactions than their U.S. counterparts. In particular, the mean borrowing volume of 7,991 requests is just 15% higher than the mean borrowing volume of 6,858 requests for the 22 college libraries.

Second, borrowing and lending unit costs are significantly higher than their U.S. counterparts. Extensive analysis confirmed that there is a statistically significant difference in the borrowing unit costs when the 11 Canadian university participants were compared with all U.S. research libraries. That difference was not attributable to volume of transactions, classification of staff positions, use of technology, use of document delivery suppliers, or to a number of other variables.

Finally, staff salaries account for 67% of the borrowing unit cost, comparable with for U.S. research and college libraries. However, staff salaries account for 83% of the lending unit cost, nearly ten percentage points higher than found in U.S. research libraries. In both the borrowing and lending operations, Canadian libraries employ fewer professionals (either supervisory or non-supervisory) and students, and rely more heavily on support staff than do U.S. research libraries.

6 COMPARISON WITH THE 1992 ARL/RLG ILL COST STUDY

The Study found that most of the 63 research libraries that participated in the 1992 ARL/RLG ILL Cost Study and this Study decreased their borrowing and lending unit costs between 1992 and 1996. Research libraries are spending less on staff as a percentage of the borrowing unit cost. Borrowing fees is the other cost category in which a significant change is evident, although it is not possible to conclude that the increase in borrowing fees directly lowered staff costs. Research libraries have not made similar shifts in their lending cost categories.

6.1 INTRODUCTION

The 1992 ARL/RLG Interlibrary Loan Cost Study reported cost information for ILL borrowing and lending operations in 76 North American research libraries. That study reported a mean borrowing unit cost of $18.62 and a mean lending unit cost of $10.93.

It is tempting, but misleading, to compare the average unit costs reported in the 1992 study with the results from this current Study because slightly different groups of libraries participated in each study. However, it is possible to compare 1992 and 1996 cost data for the 63 libraries that participated in both studies, and for which data are available.[26] The 63 participants are identified in Appendix A. Nearly all of the 63 participants recorded an increase in volume of transactions between 1992 and 1996, and many showed significant reductions in borrowing and/or lending unit costs.

6.2 VOLUME OF ACTIVITY

Fifty-nine (59) of the 63 libraries supplied data for borrowing and lending operations; four supplied data for their lending operations. Fifty-two (52) of the 59 increased their volume of borrowing between 1992 and 1996; only seven borrowed fewer items in 1996 than they did in 1992. For lending, the pattern is somewhat different: 44 libraries increased volume and 19 decreased volume.

In 1992, the 59 libraries that borrow filled on average 10,293 borrowing requests; in 1996 the same subset filled on average 14,917 borrowing requests, a 45% increase over five years. In 1992, the 63 research libraries that lend filled, on average, 26,770 lending requests; in 1996 the same group filled, on average, 27,491 requests, a three percent increase.

6.3 UNIT COSTS

Table 41 summarizes mean unit costs for the 63 research libraries that participated in both studies. Readers are reminded that the unit costs in this table vary from the often-cited findings of the 1992 study because participant groups were not identical.

For this subset, the 1996 mean borrowing unit cost is $17.82, and the 1992 mean borrowing unit cost was $16.93. For lending, the 1996 mean unit cost is $9.56,

TABLE 41

Comparison of Mean Borrowing and Lending Unit Costs for the 63 Libraries that Participated in the 1992 and 1996 Studies

	Borrowing	Lending
1992	$16.93	$10.56
1996	$17.82	$ 9.56
1996 in 1992 dollars	$15.51	$ 8.32
% change comparing constant dollars	–13%	–21%

and the 1992 mean unit cost was $10.56. However, even these comparisons are misleading because they do not account for inflation. Using $1.149 to adjust for inflation, the 1996 mean borrowing unit cost in constant dollars is $15.51, and the 1996 mean lending unit cost in constant dollars is $8.32.

Although the unadjusted mean borrowing unit cost increased, when adjusted for inflation, the mean borrowing unit cost decreased 13% ($17.82 to $15.51). For lending, the mean lending unit cost decreased 21% ($10.56 to $8.32).

Most of the 63 libraries decreased their borrowing and lending unit costs. For many, the reduction in unit costs may be due to increased volume of requests. However, other factors may also contribute to a library's reduction in unit costs: elimination of the professional supervisor position, retirement of long-term staff and hiring of replacements at a lower salary, increased reliance on student assistants, and/or increased reliance on electronic technologies and software.

More detailed analysis of borrowing and lending unit costs was not possible because 1992 institution-specific data were not available in a machine-readable format. However, since over 80% of the 1992 participants also participated in the 1996 study, this section compares the 1996 performance of the subset of 63 research libraries that participated in both studies with the 1992 performance of the 76 research libraries. **Figure 6 reveals that research libraries are spending less on staff as a percentage of the borrowing unit cost. Borrowing fees is the other cost category in which a significant change is evident, although it is not possible to conclude that the increase in borrowing fees directly lowered staff costs. Figure 7 compares lending cost categories and reveals no major shifts.**

---

[26] 1992 data for one of the 64 libraries that participated in the ARL/RLG ILL Cost Study were not available.

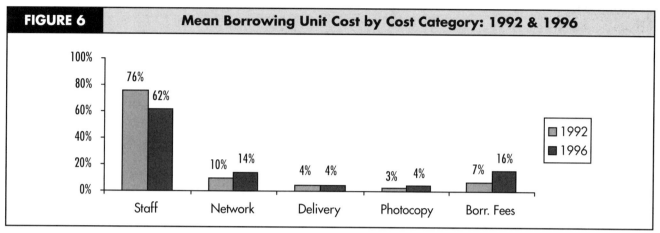

FIGURE 6 — Mean Borrowing Unit Cost by Cost Category: 1992 & 1996

* Note: For borrowing, Supplies and Equipment categories are combined with the Photocopy category.

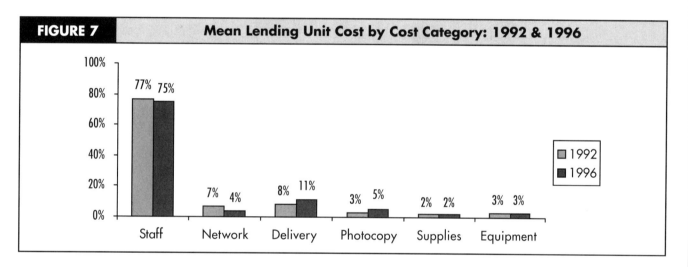

FIGURE 7 — Mean Lending Unit Cost by Cost Category: 1992 & 1996

6.4 STAFF COMPARISONS

Because staff salaries continue to represent the major portion of unit cost, Figure 8 presents the breakdown of borrowing staff by position category. It is important to remember that this section compares data from the 63 research libraries that participated in both studies with the 76 research libraries in the 1992 study.

Research libraries have increased supervisory staff (professional and support staff) from 18% to 34% of total staff cost and have decreased professional non-supervisor and support staff categories as percentages of staff cost for borrowing. These changes may be due in part to different groups of participants and in part to changes in staffing in the libraries that participated in both studies.

Figure 9 compares lending staff by position category. Research libraries increased their use of professional non-supervisors, support staff supervisors, and students, and decreased use of professional supervisors and support staff. Again, these changes may reflect the slightly different groups of participants, conscious decisions to re-deploy staff, or simply the hiring of replacement staff at lower salaries.

6.5 ESTIMATED TOTAL ILL/DD EXPENDITURES

The 1992 study estimated that all ARL libraries spent in 1992 a total of $71 million on ILL/DD activities. Of that, $26 million was spent on 1.4 million borrowing transactions and $45 million on 4.1 million lending transactions. In 1996, all ARL libraries spent $79 million on ILL transactions—$36 million on just under 2 million borrowing transactions and $43 million on 4.6 million lending transactions.

Although total ILL/DD expenditures have increased $8 million over the past five years, it is important to note that ARL libraries spent $2 million less (in real dollars) on lending activities in 1996 than in 1992.

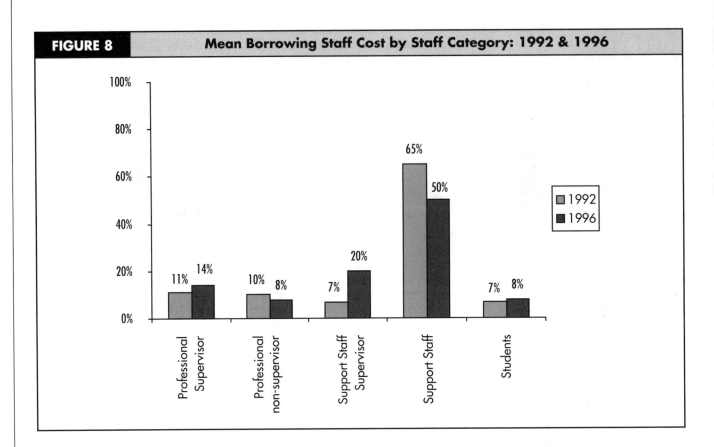

FIGURE 8 — Mean Borrowing Staff Cost by Staff Category: 1992 & 1996

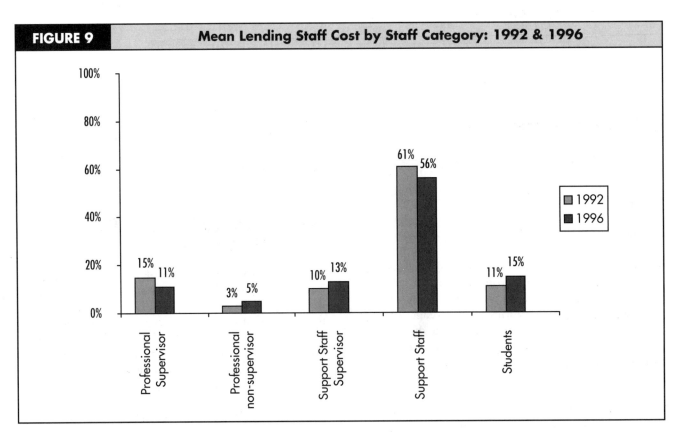

FIGURE 9 — Mean Lending Staff Cost by Staff Category: 1992 & 1996

Several possible causes can be suggested: libraries are using document delivery services rather than asking libraries to supply copies, lending operations are benefiting from local automation efforts, or lending requests are receiving less staff mediation and being processed more like circulation transactions. However, this current Study did not determine the exact cause of the $2 million decrease. In terms of constant dollars, total expenditures on ILL/DD activities have decreased by $3 million, or 4%. Table 42 compares estimates from the two studies in actual and constant dollars.

In 1992, ARL libraries spent $1,524,820,489 on salaries and wages, or 72% of all library expenditures, excluding material costs. On a unit cost basis, staff account for 77% of the cost of an ILL transaction, making ILL only slightly more labor-intensive than overall library services. Looking at these totals from a different perspective, only five percent of the approximately $1.5 billion spent on staff was dedicated to interlibrary loan services.

In 1996, ARL libraries spent $1,592,290,614 on salaries and wages, or 73% of all library expenditures, excluding material costs. In 1996, ILL/DD staff expenditures totaled $56 million, or only 3.5% of the $1.6 billion spent on all staff in research libraries. It is surprising that even though ILL transaction volumes increased significantly between 1992 and 1996, expenditures on ILL staff, as a percentage of total expenditures on all library staff, actually decreased 1.5%.

6.6 CHANGES MADE TO ILL OPERATIONS SINCE 1992

In the General Characteristics Questionnaire, research libraries that participated in the 1992 study were asked to describe changes made to ILL operations in the past five years. A total of 53 libraries listed specific changes; the remaining 11 libraries may have made changes but did not report them on the questionnaire.

Thirty (57%) libraries added staff and ten (19%) upgraded positions. Of the eight libraries (15%) that reduced the number of staff, four eliminated the professional department head position. Only one library downgraded staff position(s).

Half (49%) added or upgraded equipment, 32% added Ariel workstations, 15% upgraded network capabilities, and 15% added software. One-fifth (19%) changed borrowing or lending policies. Three libraries centralized borrowing and lending and two libraries decentralized those operations. Nine percent changed workflow or procedures and 11% changed the administrative reporting structure.

One-third (33%) increased their use of document delivery suppliers and 15% introduced patron-initiated ILL/DD requesting. Other changes reported by individual libraries include joining consortia, expanding/renovating physical space, changing the name of the department, improving workflow, changing delivery methods, improving or expanding training, and losing external funding.

Many of the changes summarized above suggest improved service, but some also suggest the potential for higher costs. It is not possible to determine the extent to which any of these changes, individually or collectively, raised or lowered unit costs or influenced other aspects of performance.

TABLE 42	Comparison of Estimated Total ILL/DD Expenditures: 1992 and 1996		
	Total	Borrowing	Lending
1992 Study	$71 million	$26 million	$45 million
1996 Study	$79 million	$36 million	$43 million
1996 in 1992 dollars	$68 million	$31 million	$37 million
% change comparing constant dollars	–8%	+19%	–18%

6.7 FINAL OBSERVATIONS

A total of 63 research libraries participated in the 1992 ARL/RLG ILL Cost Study and the 1996 ILL/DD Performance Measures Study. Most decreased borrowing and lending unit costs, a few quite dramatically, as shown on the scatter diagrams in Appendix E. Research libraries are spending less on staff as a percentage of their 1996 borrowing unit costs and are spending more on borrowing fees. On a borrowing unit cost basis, research libraries have increased their use of professional supervisors, support staff supervisors, and students, and have decreased their use of professional non-supervisors and support staff.

For lending, the breakdown of unit cost by cost categories revealed no major shifts. On a lending unit cost basis, research libraries are using fewer professional supervisors and support staff, and more professional non-supervisors, support staff supervisors, and students.

7 HIGH-PERFORMING ILL/DD OPERATIONS IN RESEARCH LIBRARIES

The average borrowing unit cost for the 25 high-performing research libraries is $11.94, 35% less than the $18.35 average borrowing unit cost for all 97 research libraries. This group recorded an average fill rate of 90%, and a 13.5 calendar day turnaround time. Ninety-three percent (93%) of their patrons are satisfied with the timeliness of service, 97% with quality, and 95% with staff.

The average lending unit cost for the 19 high-performing lenders is $7.38, 22% less than the $9.48 average lending unit cost for all research libraries. The average fill rate for the 19 best lenders is 75%, 29% higher than the average fill rate of 58% for all research libraries.

7.1 INTRODUCTION

One objective of the ILL/DD Performance Measures Study was to describe characteristics of high-performing borrowing and lending operations. The Study examined and reported performance of ILL/DD operations in research and college libraries as separate findings for two important reasons. First, there are significant differences in performance between the two types of libraries. Second, participants prefer to compare their own performance with operations in peer institutions. The Study defined a high-performing ILL/DD operation as one that fell in the top ten percent of one or more of the three borrowing measures, or one or both of the two lending measures.

Table 3 in Section 3 displays significant differences in ILL/DD performance between research and college libraries. In fact, high-performing ILL operations in research libraries are comparable to the mean performance of ILL operations in college libraries. Table 43 presents the average performance of high-performing research libraries in five performance categories. The composition of the five subgroups are not the same, that is the ten libraries with the lowest borrowing unit costs are not the same as the ten with the lowest lending unit costs. Table 43 presents the average for each of the five subgroups and shows the number of college libraries (from the group of 22 that participated in the Study) with performance equal to or better than the average of each subgroup. Because findings for user satisfaction for college and research libraries are very similar, they are not presented in this table.

As Table 43 illustrates, performance of ILL operations in some college libraries exceeds that of the high-performing ILL operations in research libraries. Four college libraries exceeded the top ten percent of research libraries in all three borrowing categories, and one of those four also exceeded the performance of the top research library lenders.

Examination of performance of college libraries falling in the top ten percent of the various measures would result in a group of two, and thus it is impossible to assure confidentiality of those two participants. In addition, it is not possible to assure confidentiality of data, especially salary data, even if data of the four college libraries described above were aggregated.

As a result, this section summarizes performance and characteristics of borrowing and lending operations of the top ten percent of research libraries without identifying the high-performing ILL operations in college libraries. The phrases "high-performing borrower," "high-performing lender," "best borrower," and "best lender" are used to describe research libraries that fall in the top ten percent of one or more performance measure.

7.2 HIGH-PERFORMING BORROWING OPERATIONS

Of the 97 research library participants, Colorado State University Libraries was the only research library that ranked in the top ten percent of all three borrowing performance measures (unit cost, fill rate, and turnaround time). The University of Chicago Libraries had a very low unit cost and a very high fill rate. Four research libraries had very low unit cost and very fast turnaround time: the University of Cincinnati, Ohio University, the University of Illinois at Chicago (UI-C) Main Library's LCS unit, and the LCS unit of UI-C's Library of the Health Sciences. (LCS, or Library Computer System, is the unit that initiates loan requests on the ILLINET Online system, the union catalog of Illinois libraries.) Most ILLINET libraries initiate requests on behalf of local patrons whereas OhioLINK libraries (such as Cincinnati and Ohio University) encourage patrons to initiate their own requests.

TABLE 43	Comparison of Performance of High-Performing Borrowing Operations	
	Mean Performance of High-Performing Research Libraries	Number of College Libraries with Equal to or Better than Performance
Borrowing unit cost	$9.76	7
Lending unit cost	$4.87	4
Borrowing turnaround time	10.2 calendar days	12
Borrowing fill rate	93%	11
Lending fill rate	78%	3

Nineteen (19) other research libraries ranked in the top ten percent of a single borrowing measure. Thus, 25 libraries ranked in the top ten percent of one or more borrowing performance measure. Data from the 25 libraries were aggregated, examined, and the summary results described below. It is important to note that some libraries with excellent performance in one category does not guarantee excellent performance in all other categories; a library with a very high borrowing fill rate may have average or below average turnaround time. However, that average or below-average performance was still used in calculating the aggregate data.

The average borrowing unit cost for the 25 high-performing research libraries is $11.94, 35% less than the $18.35 average borrowing unit cost for all 97 research libraries. This group recorded an average fill rate of 90%, and a 13.5 calendar day turnaround time. Ninety-three percent (93%) of their patrons are satisfied with the timeliness of service, 97% with quality, and 95% with staff.

Table 44 compares borrowing performance of the 25 best borrowers, the 10 research libraries with the lowest unit costs, the 97 research libraries, and the 22 college libraries. Table 45 compares borrowing unit cost by cost category. Both tables confirm that the performance of high-performing borrowers and the libraries with the lowest unit costs are comparable to the mean performance of the 22 college library participants. It is also interesting to note the significant difference in the percentage of returnable requests processed by high-performing borrowers and research libraries with very low unit costs with the percentage processed by college libraries, but the Study did not explore reasons for that variation.

TABLE 44	Comparison of High-Performing Borrowing Operations			
	25 High-Performing Borrowers	10 Research Libraries with the Lowest Borrowing Unit Costs	97 Research Libraries	22 College Libraries
Unit cost	$11.94	$6.69	$18.35	$12.08
Fill rate	90%	89%	85%	91%
Turnaround time	13.5 days	12.8 days	15.6 days	10.8 days
Average # borrowing requests	19,037	27,324	13,407	6,858
% returnables	66%	79%	51%	39%
% of borrowing to total ILL activity	43%	42%	33%	57%

TABLE 45	Comparison of Mean Borrowing Unit Costs by Cost Category			
	25 High-Performing Borrowers	10 Research Libraries with the Lowest Borrowing Unit Costs	97 Research Libraries	22 College Libraries
Staff	62%	59%	66%	62%
Network/communication	15%	16%	12%	13%
Delivery	5%	5%	4%	6%
Photocopy	0%	0%	0%	0%
Supplies	1%	1%	1%	1%
Equipment	2%	2%	3%	3%
Borrowing fees	15%	17%	14%	15%
Total	100%	100%	100%	100%

7.2.1 Staff Costs

As shown in Table 46, the 25 high-performing borrowers use fewer non-supervisory professionals, more students, and rely more on support staff for supervisory functions than do all 97 research libraries. To understand the impact of staff salaries on unit cost, additional analysis of staff unit cost was completed for the ten libraries with the very lowest borrowing unit costs. It appears that research libraries with the lowest borrowing unit costs rely more on support staff supervisors, individuals more likely to supervise and process requests, than even the group of 25 high-performing borrowers do, and certainly more than all 97 research libraries do. It is reasonable to speculate that assigning staff who supervise and process requests may result in lower unit costs than simply employing staff whose only function is supervision, but the Study did not confirm that speculation.

7.2.2 Use of Technology and Other General Characteristics

A number of similarities emerge when the general characteristics of the 25 high-performing borrowing operations are examined. ILL operations are centralized in 80% of the libraries. Just under half (44%) of ILL departments are organizationally part of the Access Services Department. Just over half (52%) of the departments are managed by support staff supervisors. Staff in 60% of the libraries work 40 hours per week. Eighty percent (80%) of professional staff are not unionized, and 50% have faculty status. Sixty percent (60%) of support staff are not unionized.

Nearly three-quarters (72%) permit patrons to place orders electronically. Just over half (52%) provide one workstation per FTE. Two thirds (64%) check union lists on OCLC; 64% use OCLC's ILL Fee Management (IFM) service; and 80% use the OCLC MicroEnhancer software. Just over half (56%) of the best borrowers use a single ILL messaging system. Of the best borrowers, 92% use OCLC for an average of 72% of their borrowing, 28% use DOCLINE for 13% of their borrowing, and 20% use RLIN for 23% of their borrowing.

Nearly three-quarters (72%) do not limit the number of requests patrons are permitted to submit at any one time. Just over half (56%) do not charge patrons for loans, and 44% do not charge patrons for photocopies. Twelve percent (12%) of all non-returnable requests are filled by document suppliers. Patrons must pick up books at the ILL office in three-quarters (75%) of the libraries, and 68% of the units mail photocopies to patrons. All institutions with undergraduates permit them to borrow. Over two-thirds (69%) use reciprocal agreements to avoid paying fees; the average borrowing fee paid is $1.71.

7.2.3 Turnaround Time

The Study asked participants to collect a sample of between 125 and 150 borrowing requests from which turnaround time was calculated. Average turnaround time for all research libraries is 15.6 calendar days, with a range for the middle 80% of between 10.2 and 22.2 calendar days. For the 11 libraries with the fastest turnaround time, turnaround time averaged 8.8 calendar days. For this same group of libraries, average turnaround time for returnables was 8.8 calendar days, and 10.5 calendar days for non-returnables.

TABLE 46	Mean Borrowing Staff Unit Costs by Staff Category			
	25 High-Performing Borrowers	10 Research Libraries with the Lowest Borrowing Unit Costs	97 Research Libraries	22 College Libraries
Professional supervisor	16%	18%	17%	28%
Professional non-supervisor	2%	1%	9%	11%
Support staff supervisor	24%	32%	20%	24%
Support staff	47%	36%	45%	28%
Students	11%	13%	9%	9%
Total	100%	100%	100%	100%

TABLE 47	Comparison of Borrowing Turnaround Time by Time Segments			
	Returnables		Non-returnables	
	10 Libraries with the Fastest Turnaround Time	10 Libraries with the Slowest Turnaround Time	10 Libraries with the Fastest Turnaround Time	10 Libraries with the Slowest Turnaround Time
Accepted at service point	.2 days	.4 days	.3 days	.7 days
Processed by ILL staff	.1 days	2.3 days	.2 days	3.5 days
Sent to first supplier	.2 days	5.0 days	.2 days	3.1 days
Received material	7.9 days	18.2 days	6.5 days	16.5 days
Notified patron	.4 days	.7 days	.2 days	.4 days
Total turnaround time	8.8 days	26.6 days	7.4 days	24.2 days

The wide variation in turnaround time between research libraries with the fastest and the slowest turnaround time is illustrated in Table 47. This table shows that research libraries with the fastest borrowing turnaround time send a request to the first potential lender/supplier in less than one calendar day, whereas libraries with the slowest turnaround time take over seven calendar days to send a request to the first supplier. The time it takes to receive materials is the other segment in which there is a noticeable difference: libraries with the fastest turnaround time receive materials ten calendars days faster than libraries with the slowest turnaround time.

The Study did not ask participants to identify reasons for delays in each of the segments measured, but the Study did identify several factors that may reduce overall turnaround time. **Eight of the nine libraries with the fastest borrowing turnaround time encourage patrons to submit requests electronically and four permit patrons to submit requests via OCLC's ILL Prism Transfer or FirstSearch-ILL link.** Electronic requesting and these OCLC ILL system features are designed to reduce delays in internal processing. Other contributing factors to efficient internal processing were not tracked in this Study, but it is reasonable to speculate that libraries with the fastest turnaround time monitor actual performance of specific lenders and choose only those with fast turnaround time. Finally, this group of libraries may have a higher percentage of requests filled by the first lender, but this Study did not ask participants for the number of libraries to which requests were sent before they were filled.

In addition, the Study did not ask participants to record the specific delivery method by which materials were received. Several factors may contribute to the

10.3 calendar day difference in the time returnables are received and the 10 calendar days for non-returnables. High-performing borrowers may use expedited delivery systems (Ariel, fax, state/regional couriers, or expedited commercial delivery couriers) to a greater extent than do libraries with the slowest turnaround time. That is, libraries with the slowest turnaround time may ask suppliers to send materials via the postal service (possibly by U.S. book rate for U.S. participants) and ask lenders to send only "rush" requests via expedited methods. In addition, libraries with the slowest turnaround time may send requests to libraries with slower-than-average internal processing. One final factor may be that libraries with very slow turnaround time may need to send requests to more potential lenders before requests are ultimately filled. Again, the Study was not able to confirm any of these speculations.

The *Interlibrary Loan Pilot Benchmark Study*, a 1994 collaborative project among ARL, the Council on Library and Information Resources, and International Systems Services Corp., concluded that turnaround time functioned as the primary performance measure in the four academic libraries studied. The current Study confirmed that ILL managers also view turnaround time as the primary performance measure. This conclusion is based on an informal survey sent to ILL managers of the 44 research libraries with a very high or very low unit cost, very fast or very slow turnaround time, and a very high or very low fill rate. Managers were asked to identify the most important criterion on which they operate their borrowing or lending operation.

As borrowers, most identified turnaround time as the criterion on which they choose lenders. However, desired and actual performance are not always the same. Of those who chose turnaround time as the most important criterion, four recorded very fast turnaround time and three recorded very slow turnaround time. The significant discrepancy between desired and actual performance for the three libraries with the slowest turnaround time suggests that these libraries may not monitor turnaround time of specific lending/supply partners. They may believe they are choosing partners with fast turnaround time, but in fact, are not.

7.2.4 Borrowing Fill Rate

The 11 research libraries with the highest fill rates reported borrowing fill rates between 93% and 98%. For returnables, the average fill rate for these 11 was 94%, with a range between 89% and 98%. The fill rate for non-returnables averaged 96%, with a range between 92% and 99%. In comparison, the ten libraries with the lowest fill rates reported an average fill rate of 69% for both returnables and non-returnables.

For the 11 libraries with the highest borrowing fill rates, borrowing unit costs ranged from $9.05 to $22.95. Seven had borrowing unit costs of less than $18.35 and four had borrowing unit costs of more than $18.35, or an average of $15.75 for all 11. For these libraries, turnaround time ranged from 9.8 to 27.0 calendar days, with seven recording turnaround times better than the average of 15.6 calendar days. For all 11, average turnaround time was 15.86 calendar days, but the median turnaround time was 12.7 calendar days.

For the 97 research library participants, there is a slight negative correlation between unit cost and borrowing fill rate. Common wisdom suggests that a library spends more money to achieve a higher fill rate. However, the Study found just the opposite—as fill rate increases, unit cost decreases. The averages

reported above confirm that libraries with the highest fill rates spend on average slightly less per transaction than all research libraries. The only certain conclusion is that spending more money, therefore having a higher unit cost, does not guarantee a higher fill rate.

7.3 HIGH-PERFORMING LENDING OPERATIONS

Of the 97 research libraries, only two libraries recorded very low lending unit costs and very high fill rates: the University of Alberta and the University of Wisconsin at Madison. An additional 17 libraries recorded either very low unit costs or very high fill rates, but not both. The characteristics of these 19 lending operations were aggregated and examined, and are summarized below.

The average lending unit cost for the 19 high-performing lenders is $7.38, 22% less than the $9.48 average lending unit cost for all research libraries. The average fill rate for the 19 best lenders is 75%, 29% higher than the average fill rate of 58% for all research libraries. Table 48 compares the performance of high-performing lenders with all research libraries, all college libraries, and the ten research libraries with the lowest lending unit cost. Table 49 compares the breakdown of lending unit cost by cost category for these four groups. These tables confirm that high-performing research library lending operations are comparable to or slightly better than the average performance of ILL operations in college libraries.

7.3.1 Staff Costs

Table 50 confirms that the ten research libraries with the very lowest lending unit costs use more student

TABLE 48	Comparison of Performance of High-Performing Lending Operations
	19 High-Performing Lenders	10 Research Libraries with the Lowest Lending Unit Costs	97 Research Libraries	22 College Libraries
Unit cost	$7.38	$3.55	$9.48	$7.25
Fill rate	75%	68%	58%	65%
Average # lending requests	29,417	39,439	27,722	5,109
% returnables	59%	53%	36%	56%
Lending as % of total	64%	63%	67%	43%

TABLE 49	Comparison of Mean Lending Unit Costs by Cost Category			
	19 High-Performing Lenders	10 Research Libraries with the Lowest Unit Costs	97 Research Libraries	22 College Libraries
Staff	79%	72%	76%	71%
Network/comm.	2%	3%	4%	6%
Delivery	7%	15%	11%	14%
Photocopy	3%	5%	4%	3%
Supplies	2%	2%	2%	2%
Equipment	7%	3%	3%	4%
Total	100%	100%	100%	100%

TABLE 50	Mean Lending Staff Unit Cost by Staff Category			
	19 High-Performing Lenders	10 Research Libraries with the Lowest Lending Unit Costs	97 Research Libraries	22 College Libraries
Professional supervisor	12%	13%	13%	19%
Professional non-supervisor	0%	0%	4%	2%
Support staff supervisor	13%	16%	13%	17%
Support staff	65%	50%	57%	38%
Students	10%	21%	13%	24%
Total	100%	100%	100%	100%

assistants and slightly less support staff in their lending operations than do either the aggregate of the 19 top lenders or the 97 research libraries. This table also confirms that high-performing lending operations in research libraries do not use professional non-supervisors in their lending operations; in contrast, professional non-supervisors account for an average of four percent of staff cost in all 97 research libraries.

7.3.2 Use of Technology and Other General Characteristics

On average, high-performing lenders spend (on a unit cost basis) just over twice as much on equipment (hardware and software) than do all 97 research libraries. Although the Study did not confirm that increased use of technology lowers unit cost, it is reasonable to speculate that increased use of technology may reduce unit cost, as technology minimizes staff involvement in some lending procedures.

Although all research libraries spend proportionately more on equipment than do college libraries, on a unit cost basis, only 53% of the 97 research libraries provide one workstation per FTE. One possible explanation is that research libraries buy more equipment, and a greater variety of equipment, for ILL departments than do college libraries, thus resulting in fewer workstations per FTE. For example, 92% of the lending operations in research libraries have a photocopy machine in the ILL office, whereas only 27% of lending operations in college libraries have a photocopy machine in the ILL department. Money spent by research libraries on photocopy machines and other equipment for the ILL department may be money redirected from the purchase of staff workstations.

Because there are more workstations per FTE in ILL operations in college libraries, it is reasonable to conclude that ILL staff in college libraries have easier access to OCLC, management software, and other tools that streamline their workflow and processing. As a result, ILL staff in college libraries may spend a greater proportion of their workday processing requests rather than working on other tasks while they are waiting for access to a workstation.

Slightly less than half (42%) of the high-performing lenders use OCLC's ILL Fee Management service; 42% use OCLC's ILL MicroEnhancer, and 68% require borrowers to enter their symbol twice, giving lenders eight, rather than four, days in which to respond to requests. Just over half (53%) of high-performing lenders use one ILL messaging system: of these, 68% use OCLC to receive 51% of their lending requests, and 26% use DOCLINE to receive 21% of their lending requests.

Nearly all (89%) of the top lenders use fax machines and 84% use Ariel to send photocopies, but the Study did not ask what percentage of requests were sent by each method. A 1996 study by the Research Libraries Group concluded that sending articles via Ariel or fax took less staff time than if sent via the U.S. mail, cost less than the U.S. mail, and decreased turnaround time for both borrowing and lending.

Of the 19 high-performing lenders, 89% of the operations are centralized; 37% of the ILL departments are included in the Access Services Department, and 37% are administratively part of the Public Services Department. Just over half (53%) of the departments are managed by support staff supervisors, and staff in 42% of the libraries work 35-hours per week. Seventy-four percent (74%) of professional staff are not unionized, and 58% of the professional staff have faculty status; 79% of the support staff are unionized.

Three-quarters (74%) of the high-performing lenders charge for filling loan requests and 89% charge for supplying photocopies. Nearly all (89%) lend to libraries outside North America, although the number of requests filled is very small. Just over half (53%) keep income in the ILL department; the average reimbursement is $3.42 per filled transaction. Most accept checks, 26% accept credit cards, 21% accept coupons, and 21% permit deposit accounts.

7.4   FINAL OBSERVATIONS

Only one research library, Colorado State University, ranked in the top ten percent of the three borrowing performance measures. Five others ranked in the top ten percent of two of the three borrowing measures.

Two research libraries, the University of Alberta and the University of Wisconsin–Madison, ranked in the top ten percent of the two lending performance measures. Seventeen other research libraries ranked in the top ten percent of one, but not both, lending measures.

In general, high-performing borrowing and lending operations in research libraries maximize use of technology and have a different mix of staff positions than do all research libraries. Several of the high-performing borrowing operations offer user-initiated ILL, which, as shown in the section on the performance of OhioLINK libraries, confirms user-initiated ILL as cost-effective.

8 CONCLUSIONS

The publication of this report signifies the completion of the analysis phase. The next step is action—action to make not incremental but astounding improvements in the performance of every library's interlibrary loan unit. We have learned from the best performers that even the best can get better, and the benefits accrue to us all.

The ILL/DD Performance Measures Study accomplished the five objectives (summarized in Section 1.2) it set out to investigate. First, the characteristics of six libraries with high and low unit costs as reported in the 1992 ARL/RLG ILL Cost Study were examined. **No common characteristics were found for either the three high unit cost libraries or the three low unit cost libraries. The lack of common characteristics confirmed that high or low unit cost is not driven by any single factor, though several similarities were found.**

The remaining four objectives were accomplished through the examination of ILL/DD operations of 97 research libraries and 22 college libraries. The Study updated cost worksheets from the 1992 ARL/RLG ILL Cost Study and collected current cost data. The Study provided new comparative data on turnaround time, fill rate, and user satisfaction. Finally, the Study examined differences among research and college libraries, identified characteristics of low-cost, high-performing ILL operations in research libraries, and suggested strategies for other libraries to improve their performance.

8.1   GENERAL FINDINGS

Research libraries spend an average of $18.35 to obtain an item for a local patron. The request takes nearly 16 calendar days to complete, and research libraries fill, on average, 85% of their borrowing requests. Research libraries spend on average $9.48 to fill a lending request and have a lending fill rate of 58%.

College libraries spend an average of $12.08 to obtain an item for a local patron. Requests take 11 calendar days to fill and the borrowing fill rate is 91%. To fill a lending request, college libraries spend an average of $7.25, with a 65% fill rate. These findings confirm that the performance of interlibrary loan operations in college libraries is better overall than ILL operations in research libraries. In three of the four performance measures, the average performance of college libraries outranked the average performance of research libraries; user satisfaction was the only measure in which the findings of the two groups were similar.

The Study also confirmed, through a regression analysis, that the difference in borrowing unit costs between college and research libraries is statistically significant. When everything else is held constant, the mean borrowing unit cost of college libraries is $5.50 less than the mean borrowing unit cost of research libraries. An

exhaustive examination of possible causal factors did not reveal any single contributing factor. The Study confirmed that the $5.50 difference is not caused by type of request (returnables/non-returnables), fill rate, turnaround time, type of staff used, volume of requests, requests per FTE, number of reciprocal agreements, length of work week, use of document delivery suppliers, etc.

One possible explanation for the cost difference between research and college libraries is that more of the requests processed by college libraries are "easier" to verify and locate than the requests handled by research libraries. Some might counter that assertion by arguing that research libraries employ staff with a range of expertise and have more resources to verify and locate "difficult" requests, and these staff skills contribute to higher costs.

A second possible reason may be that research library staff are paid more than college library staff. The *ALA Survey of Librarian Salaries 1997* [27] presents the results of a survey of nearly 1,000 U.S. libraries. Positions are grouped, and within each group, salaries presented by five library types; these five library types are further divided by region. Examination of the "Department Head/Branch Head" tables for "Four-Year College Libraries" and "University Libraries" confirmed that the mean salary paid to a department head in a college library is 19% less than a department head in a university library. "Department Head" is the group in which the ILL department head would be classified. Similar differences are noted for reference librarians (17% less), catalogers (17% less), and even more significant differences are found for directors (44% less) and deputy directors (65% less). It is important to note that the sample populations are not identical: 115 four-year colleges and 196 university libraries reported data for the ALA survey. **However, these salary differences should be tested to see if they are the underlying cause of the difference in unit costs between research and college libraries. Determining the cause for the statistically significant difference of borrowing unit costs between college and research libraries is an important area for further study.**

The Study also found a difference in unit costs between U.S. and Canadian university libraries. When ILL operations in Canadian and U.S. university libraries are compared and even when transaction volume is held constant, the mean borrowing unit cost in Canadian university libraries is $3.00 more than the mean unit cost in U.S. university libraries. A regression analysis found that

---

27 *ALA Survey of Librarian Salaries 1997.* Mary Jo Lynch, Project Director. (Chicago, IL: American Library Association, 1997): 10-12.

the difference is not statistically significant, but the Study could not identify any causes for the difference. **The Study ruled out a number of possible causes, but this also remains an area for additional study.**

The findings of the Study confirmed many of the 63 research library participants in the 1992 ARL/RLG ILL Cost Study have realized cost containment or cost reduction over the past five years. Cost containment, or processing more transactions for the same unit cost when factoring in inflation, was achieved by eight borrowing operations (14%), and seven lending operations (11%). Cost reduction, or processing more transactions for a lower unit cost, was achieved by 27 borrowing operations (46%) and 31 lending operations (49%). Thus, over the past five years approximately sixty percent (60%) of the participating research libraries have realized savings in running ILL departments.

This Study also validated findings of the ARL/RLG ILL Cost Study by confirming that the current unit costs for research libraries are within range of the findings of the 1992 study. In addition, this Study captured new and detailed information about the organization, staffing levels, use of technology, and other service and policy characteristics of ILL operations in research and college libraries.

Staff salaries account for the major portion of the unit cost for borrowing and lending. For borrowing, staff costs represent 66% of the unit cost for research libraries and 62% for college libraries. Staff costs for the lending operations are somewhat higher: 76% for research libraries and 71% for college libraries.

The Study characterized attributes of **low-cost, high performing ILL/DD operations** in research libraries. When compared with all research libraries, high-performing borrowing operations spend 35% less, fill 6% more of their requests, and obtain materials 13% faster. High-performing lending operations spend 22% less and fill 29% more lending requests than the average of all 97 research libraries. The best performance of borrowing or lending operations in research libraries is comparable to the average performance of all 22 college libraries.

8.2 IDENTIFYING STRATEGIES FOR IMPROVING LOCAL PERFORMANCE

A number of specific strategies for improving local performance have been identified throughout this report. These strategies center around three key areas: technology, staffing, and administrative issues. Many

are immediately applicable to most ILL departments, while others may require new funding, changes in staff, or administrative agreement on policy changes.

Maximizing use of **technology** is something all libraries can do. Libraries have a variety of options for allowing patrons to submit requests electronically: Web forms, email templates, OCLC's ILL Direct Request (the ISO ILL Protocol-based successor to their proprietary method), OCLC's Prism-ILL link, and ILL modules of several online local catalog systems.

Utilizing technology to manage paper files can reduce staff involvement in the process. Several software programs are available to reduce most if not all internal paper files. Many of the libraries with high-performing operations maximize use of available management software. The challenge for some ILL managers is to rely on software to track requests instead of maintaining backup paper files.

Libraries can minimize invoice generation and bill payment by putting into practice OCLC's ILL Fee Management system, IFLA vouchers, or the Electronic Fund Transfer System used by a growing number of medical libraries. Many libraries establish reciprocal, no-fee agreements to waive lending fees, such as the aptly-named LVIS (Libraries Very Interested in Sharing).

Physical and electronic delivery are other areas in which technology can play a key role. Borrowers could ask suppliers to send all articles via Ariel or fax and lenders could deliver all articles via these methods even if not requested by borrowers. For returnable materials, libraries could increase their use of expedited surface delivery services, such as UPS, FedEx, or state/regional couriers, using the electronic tracking software provided by the couriers rather than maintaining paper files.

These examples are ones that minimize staff intervention, freeing staff to perform other tasks currently not handled by software or equipment. Libraries interested in improving their ILL operations can investigate the effectiveness of new software or hardware to replace manual procedures, such as re-keying data. If software, rather than staff, transfer data from one system to another, staff time is obviously saved. With software, it may be possible to reexamine the level of staff assigned to those tasks.

A more indirect impact of the benefits of technology is exemplified by a regular plan to upgrade hardware and software. A number of libraries with high-performing borrowing and lending operations upgrade workstations on a regular basis, encourage local development of programs not commercially available, and beta test new equipment and software before they are introduced to the library marketplace. In addition, staff in high-performing operations appear to be more experimental in exploring how technology will improve their operations. Hiring staff with knowledge of technology rather than of ILL processes was a conscious decision on the part of one of the best performers.

The type of **staffing** assigned to ILL units is another area that deserves closer examination by managers of ILL operations. Data in this Study were subjected to rigorous regression analysis to identify whether the use or non-use of any specific staff category directly raised or lowered unit costs. However, no direct causal relationships were found. In spite of that unexpected finding, the Study did find positive correlations that suggest that composition of staffing, types of positions used, and even the type of supervisor increase or decrease unit costs. Nonetheless, none of the variables studied, in and of themselves, caused a change to the unit cost.

Since the regression analysis did not identify any specific causes for unit cost increases or decreases, the characteristics of low-cost, high-performing borrowing and lending operations may offer some suggestions on how to manage ILL/DD operations. Many of the high-performing operations maximize use of support staff supervisors and students, assigning students to tasks that other libraries may limit to full-time staff. Given their extensive use of student employees, training and retention are critical for high-performing libraries, but the libraries studied have found effective training solutions.

Some libraries have implemented user-initiated or unmediated ILL systems to reduce costs. Some of the research library participants that use ILLINET Online and OhioLINK were among those with the lowest unit costs and fastest turnaround times. User-initiated systems offer the potential to minimize greatly—or eliminate completely—staff processing, freeing staff to handle requests not found on those systems.

The **organization and administration** of ILL departments is another area in which change may improve service. Although Section 3.6.4 suggests that operations with decentralized borrowing and centralized lending perform slightly better than all research libraries, libraries with the very lowest costs, highest fill rates, and fastest turnaround time have centralized borrowing and lending, with one unit handling both operations. The high-performing operations are ones in which efficient workflow and procedures have been established and are reviewed on a regular basis. As an example, most of the high-performing borrowers regularly monitor performance of specific partners and change their preferred lending partners based on their findings. ILL managers of high-performing operations exhibit a curiosity about equipment, software, procedures, and policies.

Although this Study did not explicitly measure it, conversations and observations confirm that high-performing operations share a common characteristic: a strong and ongoing commitment to and support for interlibrary loan services by senior library management. Senior library administrators encourage ILL managers and staff to make changes and support them if mistakes are made. Financial assistance is also evident: equipment is purchased and budgets are established to use sources that charge or pay for expedited delivery.

8.3   APPLYING THESE STRATEGIES TO LOCAL OPERATIONS

Interlibrary loan is firmly grounded on the philosophy of reciprocity. Libraries lend because they need to borrow. A reluctance to improve local service (either as a lender or a borrower) affects other libraries. For example, a lending library may justify internally why it does not or cannot send all articles via Ariel or fax. However, it is unlikely that the staff consciously think about how that decision increases borrowers' turnaround time. The system of interlibrary loan will be improved nationally, and internationally, when all players realize the importance of their contribution to the system as a whole.

Evaluating the acceptability of current performance of local ILL/DD operations is based first on local expectations of the service. High expectations may result in a high level of service; low expectations come with more modest service goals. The Study produced a wealth of data that participants and non-participants alike can use to improve local service. As the saying goes, if we can't measure it, we can't manage it. This Study has provided a number of institution-specific and aggregate measures with which to evaluate and manage interlibrary loan services.

What are the expectations of interlibrary loan services in research and college libraries? Two common themes have been articulated in a variety of ways: the need to maximize efficiency of access to information resources, and the need to minimize costs associated with that activity. The Study identified many specific recommendations and several general strategies for improving local operations.

Strategies used by high-performing borrowing and lending operations are clearly effective in providing access to a wide range of information resources at costs that are sustainable to libraries. However, the real value in any project of this nature is the role the findings can play as a change agent for improving performance of ILL operations in all types and sizes of libraries.

Having identified the characteristics of low-cost, high-performing ILL/DD operations, ARL is planning a series of workshops to assist attendees in evaluating and adapting these performance enhancing procedures and tools for improving local service. These workshops, aimed at ILL managers and heads of public services, will provide additional details on characteristics of high-performing borrowing and lending operations. The workshops will include specific questions administrators and ILL managers can use to evaluate local operations. ARL is also developing an institution-specific process to be used by libraries to compare their local operations against those of top performers and replicate the characteristics of high-performing ILL/DD operations.

8.4   A LOOK BACK

The review of the literature on the performance of interlibrary loan services revealed an unexpected, and disappointing discovery: the performance of current ILL/DD operations may not have kept pace with the significant technical, financial, and procedural improvements introduced during the past two decades. In 1951, James G. Hodgson, Director of the Colorado A&M College Library (now Colorado State University Libraries) published a "Progress Report on a Study of Interlibrary Loan Costs." Hodgson used IBM keypunch technology to examine nearly 2,400 records from 35 libraries and union catalog centers. Although current managers might be envious of unit costs reported— approximately $1.00 to borrow an item and $0.50 to lend an item—several of his findings and observations need to be repeated.

First, borrowing was twice as expensive as lending, and those proportions are confirmed by the findings of this Study. Second, nearly 50 years ago labor costs accounted for 72.3% of the borrowing cost and 83.9% of the lending cost, both only slightly higher than the findings of the current Study. Turnaround time averaged 15.6 calendar days for requests sent to a bibliographic center for processing and 16.4 days for requests sent directly to lending libraries, also very similar to current performance of research libraries. It is disappointing that the revolutionary changes and improvements ILL managers

have incorporated into their operations over the past twenty years (the OCLC, RLIN, WLN, and DOCLINE ILL systems, automated circulation capabilities in local online catalogs, fax and Ariel technology, SAVEIT and other management software, to cite just a few examples) have not significantly reduced staff costs or improved turnaround time by any measurable degree.

8.5   AREAS FOR ADDITIONAL PRIVATE SECTOR PRODUCT DEVELOPMENT

In 1993, the Association of Research Libraries established the North American Interlibrary Loan and Document Delivery (NAILDD) Project to promote developments to maximize access to research resources while minimizing costs associated with such activities. Working with the library community, the NAILDD Project identified three short-term priority needs to enable libraries to improve their ILL/DD services in a networked environment. Through several working groups, the NAILDD Project encourages action on the part of private sector developers to create comprehensive management software, improve the ILL billing and payment process, and increase system interoperability via use of national and international standards.

Over the past five years, the private sector has responded to these needs in a variety of encouraging ways, including: OCLC's introduction of the ILL Fee Management system; The Library Corporation's development of a testbed to exchange ISO ILL Protocol-compliant messages; Research Libraries Group's incorporation of a subset of ILL Protocol messages into the Ariel software; and Ameritech's introduction of a Protocol-based resource sharing system, to mention just a few.

ILL operations have embraced many new technologies and software packages in order to improve internal workflow, but, in spite of their availability, many participants in the Study have chosen not to implement them. Participant comments confirm that many products still do not meet local needs, creating a void that yet needs to be filled by private sector vendors.

Two findings from this Study underscore the continuing need for additional technical developments by the private sector. First, the need for comprehensive management software to track ILL requests from multiple ILL utilities is confirmed in Table 27, which summarizes use of the bibliographic utilities' ILL systems. A full 40% of research libraries use more than one ILL system. At present, there is no software product that can process requests from all four bibliographic utilities. This table does not include requests generated on systems such as ILLINET Online or OhioLINK, or sent via email, fax, post, etc. Just over half of all 119 participants use locally developed software or are required to maintain paper files because of the limitations of existing commercially available software.

Second, findings from the four OhioLINK research library participants confirm the cost effectiveness of user-initiated interlibrary loan. Libraries interested in offering user-initiated ordering as a cost-effective alternative to mediated interlibrary loan are often unable to do so because their local systems do not yet support user-initiated interlibrary loan. As of early 1998 only Innovative Interfaces, Inc. offers a user-initiated ordering system fully integrated into a local online catalog, although a number of other local system vendors are developing user-initiated modules. Expediting implementation of standards-based user-initiated systems will facilitate inter-system communication.

Findings from this Study confirm the three technical priorities (comprehensive management software, financial/accounting enhancements, and standards) identified by the NAILDD Project in 1993 and underscore the ongoing need for products and services to ease the labor-intensive nature of the interlibrary loan process.

8.6 AREAS FOR FURTHER RESEARCH

From the findings of the ILL/DD Performance Measures Study, a series of recommendations for additional research or study emerged. The potential directions for future research are as varied as they are numerous. The following recommendations first appeared in earlier sections of this report. This Study suggests follow-up examination of:

- the variation in fill rates for returnable and non-returnable requests;

- turnaround time from the perspective of the lender;

- the extent to which restrictive borrowing or lending policies contribute to the overall fill rate;

- reasons why individuals at institutions with high-performing borrowing operations do not use interlibrary loan services;

- the relationship between turnaround time and use of document delivery suppliers, and why increased use of document suppliers does not appear to reduce turnaround time;

- the costs and performance of OhioLINK user-initiated transactions;

- the causal reasons why college libraries have statistically significant lower unit costs; and

- the causal reasons why Canadian university libraries have higher borrowing unit costs than university libraries in the U.S.

Additional research is needed on several aspects of interlibrary loan performance. This Study is the first to track comprehensive turnaround time on a North American scale, but this investigation defined turnaround time from the perspective of the borrowing library. One area for further study should focus on the lending library's internal performance. How quickly does a lending library respond to requests by sending the item or a negative response? How does a lending library's turnaround time compare with the advertised or actual turnaround time of a document supplier?

The General Characteristics Questionnaire asked borrowers if they used union lists to verify whether potential lenders own the requested volume and/or issue. Use of union lists varies. Of those who use OCLC, 62% of the research libraries with high-performing borrowing operations check union lists prior to choosing potential lenders. Although over 90% of all borrowers in the Study check union lists, the Study did not ask participants to indicate the extent to which checking is done. Increased use of union lists may increase lenders' fill rates because lenders would not receive requests for material in volumes and/or issues they do not own, but the currency of the union lists needs to be maintained for borrowers to feel it is cost-effective for them to check the lists. An area for further research is whether the additional cost of maintaining up-to-date union lists would outweigh the reduction in unit cost for either the borrower or lender, or for the ILL system as a whole.

This Study did not evaluate the efficiency of internal operations. However, the wide range in borrowing and lending requests processed per FTE presented in Section 3.6.3 suggests that some ILL departments may be more productive than others. In a 1989 report of ILL workload and staffing patterns in ARL libraries, Pat Weaver-Meyers measured productivity, or efficiency, using a ratio of total requests processed to staff FTE ratio. Implicit in Weaver-Meyer's discussion is the assumption that the higher ratio of requests processed per staff, the more productive the operation. A library may have very restrictive lending policies or high lending charges and thus rejects a high percentage of lending requests, but fill most of those that they do accept for processing. Is that library more productive than a library that accepts all incoming lending requests but rejects many requests for various reasons? The first library has a high fill rate but a low productivity rate; the second has a low fill rate but a high productivity rate. Further study is needed on the volume of requests filled to FTE ratio and to assess how best to measure the productivity of interlibrary loan operations.

Another issue that lends itself to further investigation in this area is the stagnation of lending fill rates for research libraries during the past decade. Is a 60% lending fill rate the best research libraries can do, or are there new strategies that will increase the lending fill rate? What will it take for research libraries with fill rates of less than the mean of 58% to increase their fill rate? Reexamination of lending policies and development of an economic model that creates incentives to lend are two possible strategies that should be investigated further.

This Study did not track costs for each of the steps of the borrowing or lending process. The Study was not designed to measure the cost of verifying, data input and maintenance, stack retrieval, photocopying, returning books, etc. The Study calculated the cost of a filled borrowing and lending transaction, but did not attempt to disaggregate the unit cost into the amount spent on each step of the borrowing or lending process. Understanding costs associated with each step of the process would help library managers identify cost-effective alternatives, and thus is an area recommended for additional investigation.

Finally, this Study was not designed to measure the performance of ILL departments in public or special libraries. This Study did not attempt to measure the overall cost to the library community, or the cost to the larger institutions that support libraries that use other libraries to obtain materials rather than document delivery suppliers. The findings on the performance of lenders/suppliers should not be generalized to other kinds of document delivery services beyond libraries. The economics and performance of using document delivery suppliers in place of other lending libraries is an area ripe for additional study.

8.7 RECOMMENDATIONS FOR IMPROVING MEASUREMENT AND LOCAL PERFORMANCE

A project of this scope is bound to develop specific recommendations for improvements in measuring the performance of interlibrary loan services as well as recommendations for changes to institution-specific ILL/DD practices. The following recommendations are included in this report.

8.7.1 Recommendations for Measuring the Performance of ILL/DD Services

Requests for "locally owned materials" should *not* be counted as filled borrowing requests. This recommendation is based on how high-performing borrowing operations count requests for materials locally owned.

Reaching national agreement on counting strategies for filled and unfilled requests generated on all online ILL systems would enable ILL managers to use statistical reports generated by those systems with confidence that ILL requests are being counted consistently.

The Study did not measure turnaround time for non-returnables in hours, but future investigations may benefit from tracking non-returnables in hours as well as days given increased use of electronic delivery technologies and/or access to full-text/full-image documents.

8.7.2 Recommendations for Improving Institution-Specific Practices

Libraries receiving fewer than 25% of their requests within seven days and fewer than 80% within four weeks should review their procedures to see how performance can be improved.

Libraries should measure their borrowing fill rate on a regular basis and should target a fill rate of not less than 95%. Libraries with a "first attempt success rate" below 80% or "second attempt success rate" below 90% should review their borrowing procedures to improve performance.

Overall, turnaround time will be faster if lenders check their shelves only one time and then forward requests to the next library/supplier rather than re-checking shelves over the course of several days (and not finding the needed item on subsequent searches) before forwarding unfilled requests to other libraries.

8.8 ONE FINAL THOUGHT

The ARL ILL/DD Performance Measures Study identified a handful of operations that chart new ways to manage interlibrary loan operations. The challenge is to spread awareness of the potential for improvements and develop strategies for replicating the best practices.

APPENDICES

APPENDIX A: LIST OF PARTICIPANTS

The follow charts list the participants in the ILL/DD Performance Measures Study.

RESEARCH LIBRARIES	1992 ARL/RLG ILL Cost Study Participant	Big Twelve Plus Participant	Submitted Cost Data	Submitted Fill Rate Data	Submitted Turnaround Time/User Satisfaction Sample	Number of Sample Requests Completed	Number of Requests Still in Process	Number of User Satisfaction Surveys Returned
Alabama			Y	Y	Y	107	6	21
Alberta			Y	Y	Y	172	77	39
Arizona	Y		Y	Y	Y	108	10	78
Arizona State	Y		Y	Y	Y	132	7	52
Arkansas	Y	Y	Y	Y	Y	78	2	68
Brigham Young	Y		Y	Y				
British Columbia–Main	Y		Y	Y	Y	101	2	64
British Columbia–Biomedical			Y	Y	Y	100	2	70
Cal–Berkeley	Y		Y	Y	Y	191	10	46
Cal–Irvine			Y	Y	Y	139	9	71
Cal–Riverside			Y	Y	Y	136	9	80
Cal–San Diego			Y	Y	Y	83	1	56
Center for Research Libraries	Y		Y	Y				
Chicago			Y	Y	Y	149	1	92
CISTI	Y		Y	Y	Y	75	25	46
Cincinnati–Main			Y	Y	Y	181	16	75
Cincinnati–Health Sciences			Y	Y				
Colorado	Y	Y	Y	Y	Y	141	9	64
Colorado State	Y	Y	Y	Y	Y	13	0	17
Columbia	Y		Y	Y	Y	146	1	58
Connecticut	Y		Y	Y	Y	184	2	133
Dartmouth	Y		Y	Y	Y	135	8	84
Duke	Y		Y	Y	Y	121	11	70
Emory			Y	Y	Y	138	6	49
Florida	Y		Y	Y				
Florida State	Y		Y	Y	Y	114	6	60
Georgetown	Y		Y	Y	Y	154	2	78

RESEARCH LIBRARIES	1992 ARL/RLG ILL Cost Study Participant	Big Twelve Plus Participant	Submitted Cost Data	Submitted Fill Rate Data	Submitted Turnaround Time/User Satisfaction Sample	Number of Sample Requests Completed	Number of Requests Still in Process	Number of User Satisfaction Surveys Returned
Georgia			Y	Y	Y	149	1	88
Harvard			Y	Y	Y	137	4	60
Houston	Y		Y	Y	Y	135	8	68
Illinois–Chicago Main–ILL	Y		Y	Y	Y	136	7	61
UIC–Main–LCS	Y		Y	Y	Y	178	38	71
UIC–LHS–ILL	Y		Y	Y	Y	169	3	76
UIC–LHS–LCS			Y	Y	Y	160	5	68
Illinois–Urbana	Y		Y	Y	Y	133	6	72
Indiana	Y		Y	Y	Y	174	6	83
Iowa State	Y	Y	Y	Y	Y	74	2	69
Johns Hopkins	Y		Y	Y	Y	151	0	89
Kansas	Y	Y	Y	Y	Y	128	0	96
Kent State			Y	Y	Y	139	1	47
Laval–Main	Y		Y	Y	Y	34	93	35
Laval–Science			Y	Y	Y	116	14	106
Library of Congress	Y		Y	Y				
Linda Hall		Y	Y	Y				
Louisiana State			Y	Y	Y	130	13	105
McGill–Main	Y		Y	Y	Y	376[1]	22	299
McGill–Health Sciences			Y	Y	Y	376	22	299
McGill–Phy Sci Eng			Y	Y	Y	376	22	299
McMaster	Y		Y	Y	Y	141	6	66
Manitoba	Y		Y	Y	Y	131	3	72
Massachusetts			Y	Y	Y	140	6	110
MIT–ILL	Y		Y	Y	Y	145	4	93
MIT–Document Delivery	Y		Y	Y				
Miami			Y	Y	Y	152	4	108
Michigan	Y		Y	Y	Y	94	0	44

[1] A total of 376 borrowing requests were submitted by the three McGill libraries but the forms did not indicate the specific ILL operation that generated the requests. As a result, the totals are reported in the aggregate for all three ILL units.

RESEARCH LIBRARIES	1992 ARL/RLG ILL Cost Study Participant	Big Twelve Plus Participant	Submitted Cost Data	Submitted Fill Rate Data	Submitted Turnaround Time/User Satisfaction Sample	Number of Sample Requests Completed	Number of Requests Still in Process	Number of User Satisfaction Surveys Returned
Minnesota–Main			Y	Y	Y	172	6	63
Minnesota–Bio Medical			Y	Y	Y	83	2	48
Missouri	Y	Y	Y	Y	Y	129	8	68
National Lib. of Canada	Y		Y	Y	Y	94	0	81
National Lib. of Medicine	Y		Y	Y				94
Nebraska	Y	Y	Y	Y	Y	110	9	116
New York State	Y		Y	Y	Y	129	0	
New York Univ.			Y	Y	Y	121	2	61
North Carolina			Y	Y	Y	123	17	82
North Carolina State–Main	Y		Y	Y	Y	121	0	82
North Carolina State–Vet Med			Y	Y				
Notre Dame	Y		Y	Y	Y	88	15	57
Ohio Univ.			Y	Y	Y	178	1	92
Ohio State	Y		Y	Y	Y	119	4	41
Oklahoma	Y	Y	Y	Y	Y	71	0	20
Oklahoma State		Y	Y	Y				
Oregon			Y	Y	Y	150	0	68
Pennsylvania	Y		Y	Y				
Pennsylvania State	Y		Y	Y	Y	131	0	37
Pittsburgh			Y	Y	Y	88	2	55
Purdue	Y		Y	Y	Y	125	0	78
Rice	Y		Y	Y	Y	140	0	111
Rochester	Y		Y	Y	Y	143	5	107
Rutgers	Y		Y	Y	Y	139	1	80
Smithsonian			Y	Y	Y	125	1	52
South Carolina	Y		Y	Y	Y	232	7	69
Southern Illinois	Y	Y	Y	Y	Y	165	15	85
Syracuse	Y		Y	Y	Y	148	1	24
Temple	Y		Y	Y				
Tennessee	Y		Y	Y	Y	121	0	33

RESEARCH LIBRARIES	1992 ARL/RLG ILL Cost Study Participant	Big Twelve Plus Participant	Submitted Cost Data	Submitted Fill Rate Data	Submitted Turnaround Time/User Satisfaction Sample	Number of Sample Requests Completed	Number of Requests Still in Process	Number of User Satisfaction Surveys Returned
Texas	Y	Y	Y	Y	Y	98	1	15
Texas A & M	Y	Y	Y	Y	Y	157	3	104
Vanderbilt	Y		Y	Y	Y	137	13	65
Virginia	Y		Y	Y	Y	121	0	63
Va. Tech	Y		Y	Y	Y	145	0	12
Washington State			Y	Y	Y	163	6	84
Washington Univ.	Y		Y	Y	Y	105	5	83
Wayne State	Y		Y	Y	Y	125	9	36
Wisconsin	Y		Y	Y	Y	139	10	77
Wyoming	Y	Y	Y	Y	Y	128	2	32
Yale	Y		Y	Y	Y	144	0	51
York			Y	Y	Y	153	10	69
COLLEGE LIBRARIES								
Agnes Scott			Y	Y	Y	83	9	36
Albion			Y	Y	Y	133	2	55
Augustana			Y	Y	Y	142	4	98
Bucknell			Y	Y	Y	112	1	47
Claremont Colleges			Y	Y				
Colgate			Y	Y	Y	135	1	66
Connecticut College			Y	Y	Y	96	0	91
Davidson			Y	Y	Y	97	3	
Earlham			Y	Y	Y	84	1	35
Franklin & Marshall			Y	Y	Y	49	2	51
Macalester			Y	Y	Y	87	1	57
Middlebury			Y	Y	Y	122	2	
Occidental			Y	Y	Y	17	0	17
Reed			Y	Y	Y	127	1	41
St. Johns			Y	Y	Y	145	0	53
Skidmore			Y	Y				
Smith			Y	Y	Y	151	0	58
Swarthmore			Y	Y	Y	126	1	31
Union			Y	Y	Y	97	5	29
Univ. of the South			Y	Y	Y	146	2	110
Wellesley			Y	Y	Y	137	4	102
Wheaton			Y	Y	Y	152	0	55

APPENDIX B: SUMMARY OF THE FINDINGS OF THE FOUR PERFORMANCE MEASURES: RESEARCH LIBRARIES

ILL Volume & Performance Measures	Research Libraries, 1996					
	Mean	Median	10th percentile	25th percentile	75th percentile	90th percentile
Total Transactions						
Total	40,571	30,131	12,967	20,245	46,246	69,124
Borrowing	13,407	11,365	3,457	7,354	16,818	25,263
Lending	27,722	19,105	6,893	10,889	29,174	47,974
Unit Cost						
Borrowing	$18.35	$16.63	$9.76	$13.04	$20.60	$27.84
Lending	$ 9.48	$ 8.14	$4.87	$ 6.25	$10.28	$16.34
Fill Rate						
Borrowing	85%	86%	75%	80%	91%	93%
Returnables	83%	86%	66%	78%	90%	95%
Non-returnables	86%	88%	71%	81%	92%	97%
Lending	58%	57%	43%	48%	67%	78%
Returnables	58%	55%	41%	51%	69%	79%
Non-returnables	58%	56%	45%	48%	70%	77%
Turnaround Time						
Total	15.6 days	14.9 days	10.2 days	12.5 days	18.0 days	22.0 days
Returnables	16.9 days	16.3 days	10.4 days	13.2 days	19.7 days	25.8 days
Non-returnables	14.9 days	13.8 days	9.8 days	11.7 days	17.0 days	22.4 days
User Satisfaction						
Timeliness	94%	95%	88%	92%	97%	99%
Quality	97%	97%	94%	96%	99%	100%
Staff	95%	96%	85%	91%	100%	100%
User Paid	8%	2%	0%	0%	6%	31%
Amount Paid	$6.95	$4.75	$2.05	$3.19	$9.04	$13.60
Willing to Pay	$2.71	$2.25	$1.43	$1.75	$3.50	$ 4.77

APPENDIX C: SUMMARY OF THE FINDINGS OF THE FOUR PERFORMANCE MEASURES: COLLEGE LIBRARIES

ILL Volume & Performance Measures	College Libraries, 1996					
	Mean	Median	10th percentile	25th percentile	75th percentile	90th percentile
Total Transactions						
Total	11,968	9,912	5,449	7,859	14,618	19,503
Borrowing	6,858	5,454	2,448	4,269	8,575	13,645
Lending	5,109	4,305	2,049	3,181	6,199	7,880
Unit Cost						
Borrowing	$12.08	$11.16	$6.39	$8.70	$14.51	$18.50
Lending	$ 7.25	$ 6.47	$4.75	$5.32	$ 8.86	$10.08
Fill Rate						
Borrowing	91%	92%	85%	89%	94%	97%
Returnables	90%	92%	81%	88%	93%	97%
Non-returnables	91%	93%	72%	86%	93%	97%
Lending	65%	66%	54%	57%	74%	87%
Returnables	65%	68%	40%	57%	75%	89%
Non-returnables	63%	64%	33%	56%	74%	87%
Turnaround Time						
Total	10.8 days	9.5 days	6.7 days	7.6 days	12.9 days	16.9 days
Returnables	11.4 days	10.9 days	6.6 days	8.6 days	13.9 days	18.0 days
Non-returnables	10.4 days	8.4 days	6.3 days	7.5 days	12.0 days	16.6 days
User Satisfaction						
Timeliness	92%	95%	84%	92%	97%	99%
Quality	98%	98%	94%	96%	100%	100%
Staff	98%	100%	94%	97%	100%	100%
User Paid	10%	2%	0%	0%	6%	28%
Amount Paid	$6.50	$5.24	$0.28	$0.91	$7.94	$14.00
Willing to Pay	$2.15	$1.96	$0.89	$1.02	$2.97	$ 3.32

APPENDIX D: UNIT COSTS IN CANADIAN CURRENCY

Section 5 includes three tables (32, 34, 35) with data on performance of the 13 Canadian participants, but with unit costs expressed in U.S. currency to allow for comparison with U.S. libraries. To facilitate interpretation by Canadian participants, these tables are reproduced again, but with unit costs reported in Canadian dollars.

TABLE 32A	Performance of Canadian Research Libraries in Canadian Dollars, 1996			
	10th percentile	Mean	Median	90th percentile
Total Transactions	8,797	51,453	22,605	99,102
Borrowing	1,209	7,991	7,319	13,881
Returnables	280	2,848	2,813	5,816
Non-returnables	803	5,143	2,714	23,692
Lending	5,021	43,463	14,725	69,732
Returnables	1,033	8,281	7,358	17,652
Non-returnables	2,488	35,266	10,533	52,080
Unit Cost				
Borrowing	$21.64	$39.22	$27.04	$74.84
Lending	$ 8.52	$13.54	$11.72	$20.00
Fill Rate				
Borrowing	76%	83%	85%	98%
Lending	62%	77%	79%	94%
Turnaround Time				
Total	12.8 days	17.5 days	16.2 days	23.6 days
Returnables	16.2 days	20.5 days	19.7 days	26.8 days
Non-returnables	10.8 days	16.2 days	13.8 days	21.9 days
User Satisfaction				
Timeliness	88%	93%	95%	96%
Quality	95%	98%	97%	100%
Staff	84%	97%	99%	100%
User Paid	0%	32%	30%	64%
Amount Paid	$0.00	$8.97	$5.64	$10.01
Willing to Pay	$2.00	$4.07	$3.19	$ 7.92

TABLE 34A	Mean Borrowing and Lending Unit Costs by Cost Category: Canadian Participants in Canadian Dollars	
	Borrowing	Lending
Staff	$26.37	$11.15
ILL Staff	$24.76	$ 8.69
Staff in other depts.	$ 1.61	$ 2.46
Network/communication	$ 2.94	$ 0.34
Delivery	$ 0.84	$ 0.89
Photocopying	$ 0.10	$ 0.30
Supplies	$ 0.26	$ 0.26
Equipment	$ 2.15	$ 0.60
Borrowing fees	$ 6.56	n/a
Total	$39.22	$13.54

TABLE 35A	Comparison of Mean Borrowing and Lending Unit Costs in Canadian Dollars		
	13 Canadian Libraries	84 U.S. Research Libraries	22 U.S. College Libraries
Borrowing	$39.22	$22.69	$16.44
Lending	$13.54	$12.78	$ 9.87

APPENDIX E: HIGH-PERFORMING BORROWING AND LENDING OPERATIONS

HIGH-PERFORMING BORROWING OPERATIONS

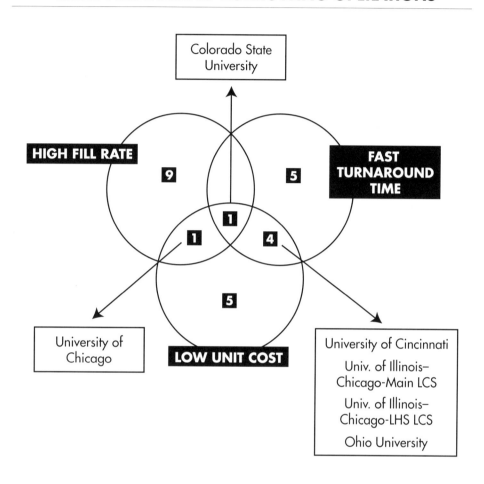

HIGH-PERFORMING LENDING OPERATIONS

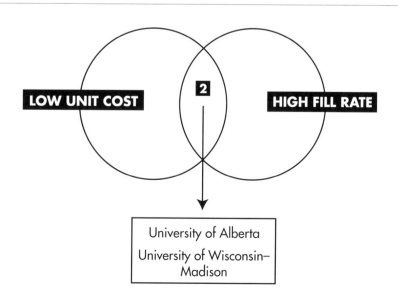

APPENDIX F: SCATTER DIAGRAMS

To assure confidentiality of the college libraries, all scatter diagrams with college library volume of transactions are excluded from this section.

Research Libraries

F1	Borrowing Volume vs. Unit Cost
F2	Borrowing Fill Rate vs. Unit Cost
F3	Borrowing Volume vs. Fill Rate
F4	Borrowing Volume vs. Turnaround Time
F5	Borrowing Fill Rate vs. Turnaround Time
F6	Borrowing Unit Cost vs. Turnaround Time
F7	Lending Volume vs. Unit Cost
F8	Lending Volume vs. Fill Rate
F9	Lending Fill Rate vs. Unit Cost

College Libraries

F10	Borrowing Fill Rate vs. Unit Cost
F11	Borrowing Fill Rate vs. Turnaround Time
F12	Borrowing Unit Cost vs. Turnaround Time
F13	Lending Fill Rate vs. Unit Cost

Comparison of 1992 and 1996 Studies: Research Libraries

F14	Change in Borrowing Unit Cost vs. Volume
F15	Change in Lending Unit Cost vs. Volume

F1   BORROWING VOLUME OF TRANSACTIONS VS. UNIT COST: Research Libraries

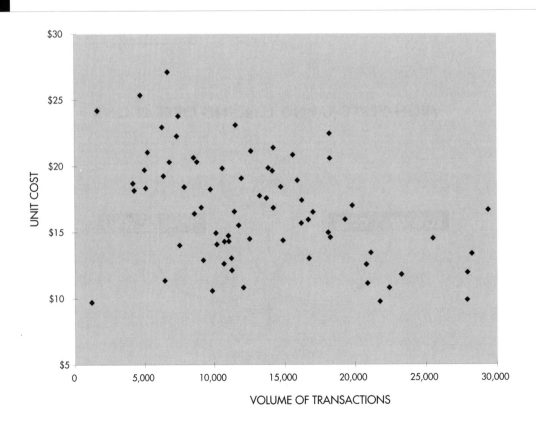

F2

BORROWING FILL RATE VS. UNIT COST: Research Libraries

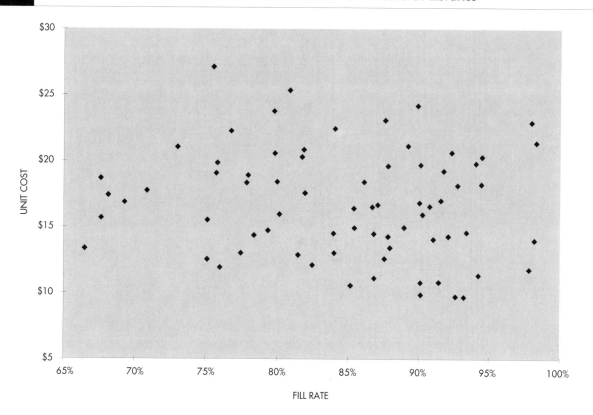

F3

BORROWING VOLUME OF TRANSACTIONS VS. FILL RATE: Research Libraries

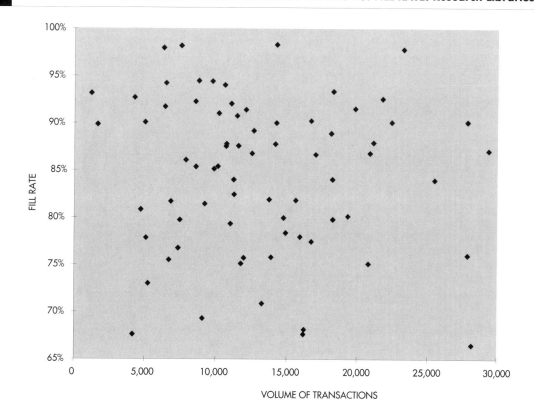

F4   **BORROWING VOLUME OF TRANSACTIONS VS. TURNAROUND TIME: Research Libraries**

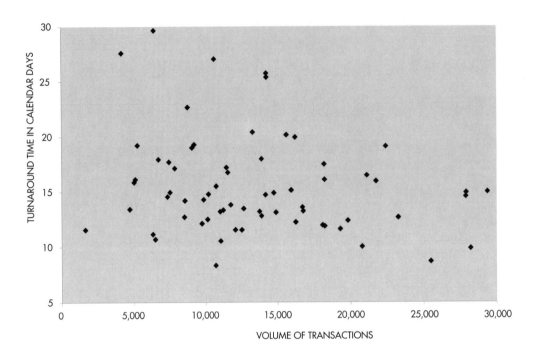

F5   **BORROWING FILL RATE VS. TURNAROUND TIME: Research Libraries**

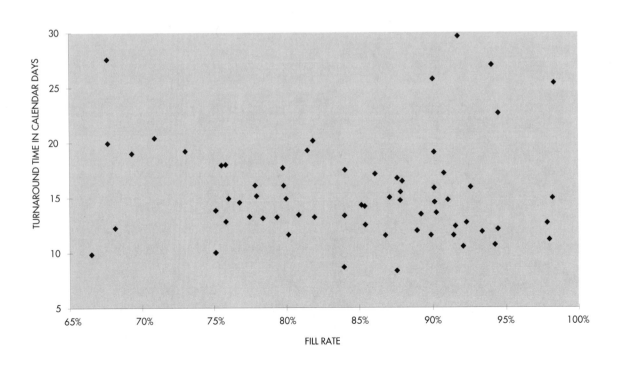

F6   **BORROWING UNIT COST VS. TURNAROUND TIME: Research Libraries**

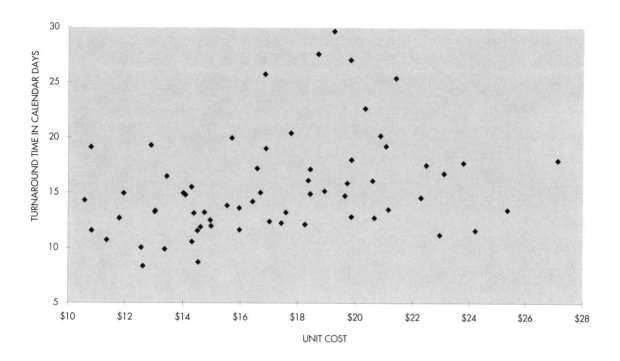

F7   **LENDING VOLUME OF TRANSACTIONS VS. UNIT COST: Research Libraries**

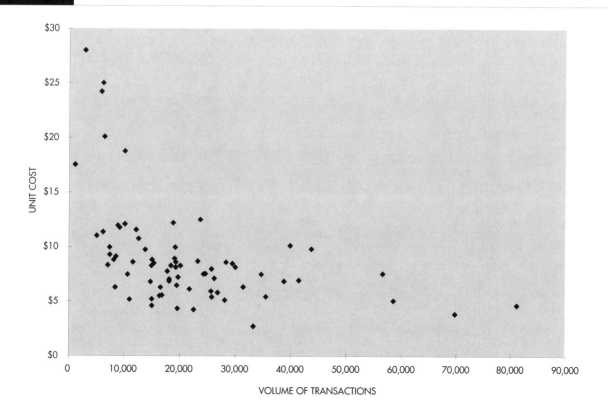

F8   LENDING VOLUME OF TRANSACTIONS VS. FILL RATE: Research Libraries

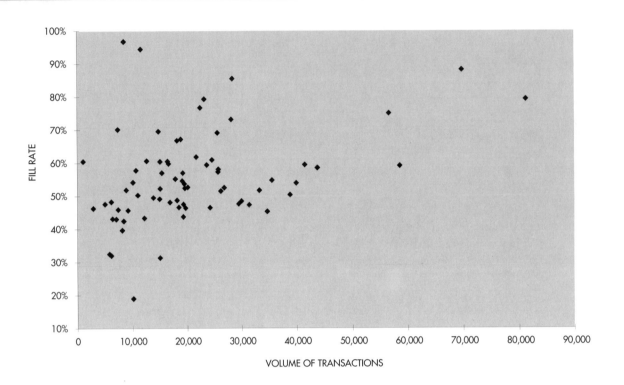

F9   LENDING FILL RATE VS. UNIT COST: Research Libraries

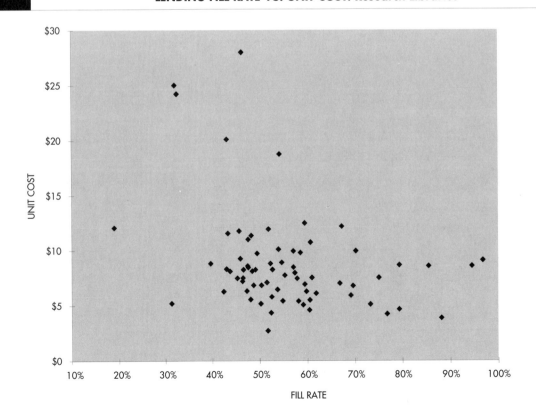

F10   BORROWING FILL RATE VS. UNIT COST: College Libraries

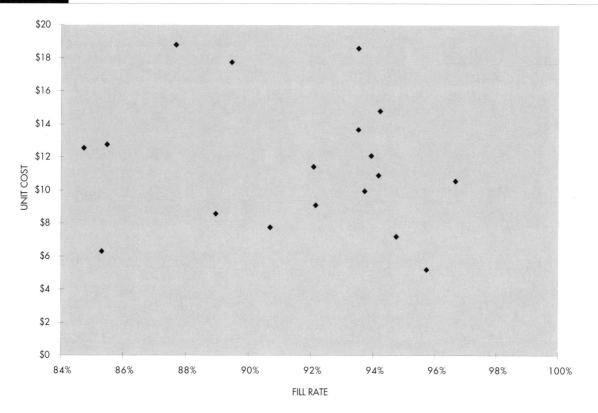

F11   BORROWING FILL RATE VS. TURNAROUND TIME: College Libraries

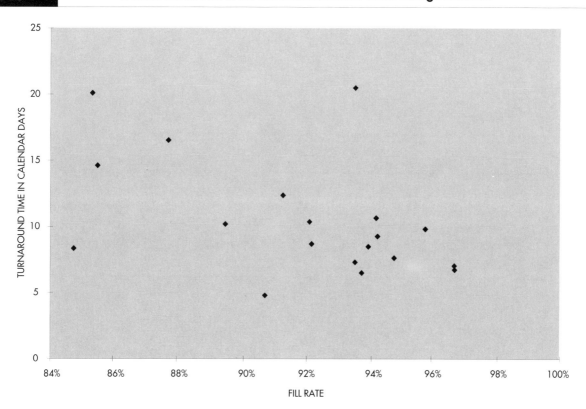

F12   **BORROWING UNIT COST VS. TURNAROUND TIME: College Libraries**

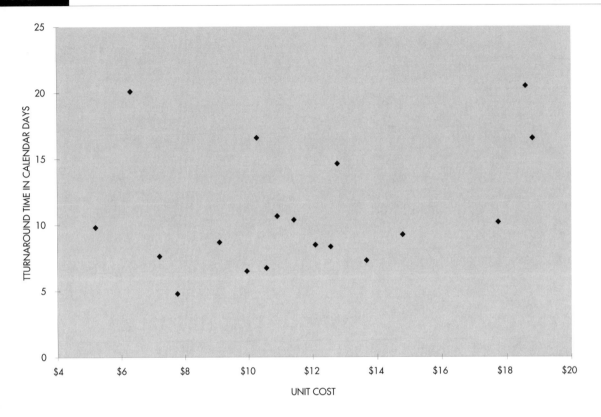

F13   **LENDING FILL RATE VS. UNIT COST: College Libraries**

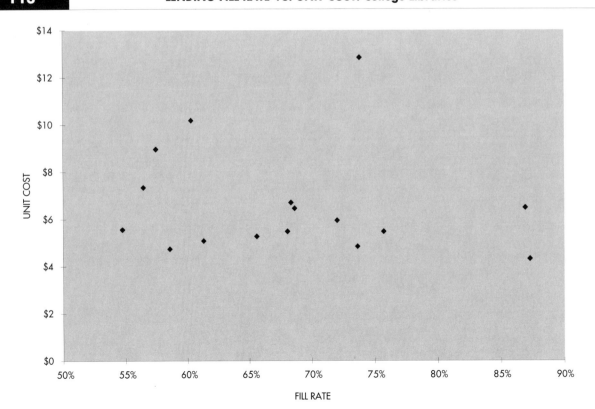

F14

CHANGE IN BORROWING UNIT COST VS. CHANGE IN VOLUME OF TRANSACTIONS: 1992 and 1996

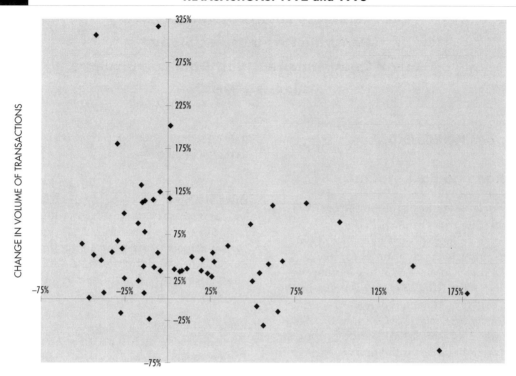

CHANGE IN UNIT COST

F15

CHANGE IN LENDING UNIT COST VS. CHANGE IN VOLUME OF TRANSACTIONS: 1992 and 1996

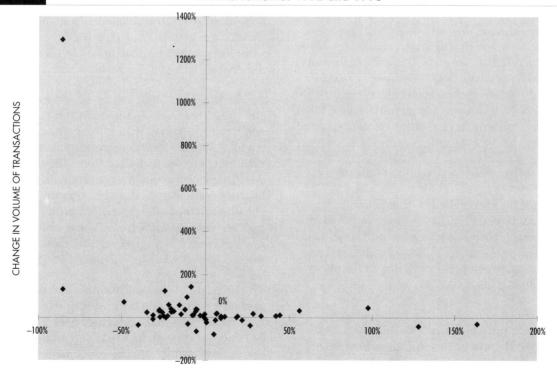

CHANGE IN UNIT COST

APPENDIX G: GENERAL INSTRUCTIONS

ARL Interlibrary Loan/Document Delivery
Performance Measures Study
General Questionnaire & Cost Data Component
August 1996

PART ONE: BACKGROUND

I. Introduction and Background

In 1992, the Association of Research Libraries (ARL) and the Research Libraries Group (RLG) collaborated in a joint project to collect detailed information on 1991 costs incurred by research libraries for interlibrary loan (ILL) transactions. The results of that project were reported in the *ARL/RLG Interlibrary Loan Cost Study: A Joint Effort by the Association of Research Libraries and the Research Libraries Group* (Washington, DC: Association of Research Libraries, 1993). Findings from that study indicated that a research library spends an average of $18.62 to borrow a document or receive a photocopy, and $10.93 to lend a document or supply a photocopy to another library. Thus, the mean cost of a filled ILL transaction for research libraries is $29.55.

In 1995, ARL received a grant from The Andrew W. Mellon Foundation to study the performance of ILL/DD operations in research and college libraries. The ILL/DD Performance Measures Study builds on the original cost study and is designed in two phases. Using data from the original cost study, Phase One examines in detail the characteristics of six libraries from the 1992 study, three with high unit cost and three with low. Phase Two collects data on turnaround time, fill rate, and user satisfaction, in addition to updated cost data.

Phase Two has been designed to collect data on additional performance measures for several reasons. The first is to place the cost of the ILL transaction into a larger context. Does a library with a high unit cost provide better service than one with a low unit cost? Incorporating other performance measures with cost data will provide a more comprehensive view of the effectiveness of the ILL process.

The second phase will collect data from college as well as research libraries. Phase Two will also test the hypothesis that ILL operations in college libraries are less expensive than those in research libraries. Again, the inclusion of additional measurements will result in a more detailed comparison of ILL services in research and college libraries.

Finally, Phase Two of the ILL/DD Performance Measures Study will offer participants a larger framework in which to compare their services with other libraries, either by type or geography. This study will also enable the seventy-six participants in the first study to compare current costs with their original data, in part to provide an opportunity to determine the cost effectiveness of changes in local services.

Each of the performance measures in Phase Two will be studied separately. This questionnaire focuses on ILL costs. The original cost study questionnaire has been revised to clarify questions that may have been difficult to interpret. The major difference between the two instruments is the inclusion of questions on returnables and non-returnables for borrowing and lending. One of the underlying goals of the ARL/RLG ILL Cost Study is to provide management data on whether to use document delivery suppliers rather than interlibrary loan to obtain copies of journal articles. That goal was not achieved because the instrument did not differentiate borrowing requests between returnables and non-returnables.

As with the original, this study focuses exclusively on costs directly associated with interlibrary borrowing and lending. Costs of major library functions such as circulation, collection development, acquisitions, and cataloging are not included. General overhead costs are specifically excluded. Both studies recognize that libraries require collections in order to share, but libraries will incur the costs of acquiring and maintaining collection regardless of whether or not they engage in interlibrary lending. Therefore, these costs are considered indirect and are excluded from this study.

The objective of the cost study portion of Phase Two is to collect unit data on borrowing and lending costs, for both returnables and non-returnables. Data will again be collected on staff, network/communications, delivery, photocopying, supplies, equipment/software/maintenance, borrowing fees, and reimbursement income. These results will be combined with data on fill rate, turnaround time, and user satisfaction in order to identify the characteristics of an effective interlibrary loan operation. This study will track institutional costs, rather than just direct library expenses as may have been reported in the first study.

As with the first cost study, ARL again ensures confidentiality of responses. Data collected will be reported in the aggregate only and will not be made available for comparison on a library-to-library basis. However, each participant will be provided with an institution-specific report of its costs and other performance measures.

II. Definitions

The following definitions are used in this study.

Administrative Head: The administrative head of the overall ILL operations and the one assigned policy-making and planning responsibilities. Most ILL operations will have one administrative head and others who may have supervisory responsibility for lending or borrowing. Do not include support staff who supervise students or have day-to-day operational responsibility for either borrowing or lending. Also known as Department Head, or in the previous Cost Study, Professional Supervisor.

Borrowing: The process of obtaining materials (books, photocopies, etc.) for individuals affiliated with the institution.

DD: Document Delivery. For this study, document delivery is defined as the purchase of non-returnables from a company or service that supplies documents for a fee. Examples include UnCover, ISI, UMI, EBSCOdoc, etc. Documents purchased from libraries with document delivery services, including fee-based services such as MITS and RICE, are not included in this definition.

FTE: Full-time equivalent staff. All staff time is converted to a portion of full-time equivalent. A full-time staff member working only in ILL is 1 FTE. A staff with a half-time assignment in ILL and half in the Reference Department is to be considered 50% FTE for this study.

ILL: Interlibrary Loan. The library operation that obtains materials for its patrons and provides locally owned materials to other libraries and individuals.

Lending: The process of sending materials (books, photocopies) owned by the institution to another library.

Loans: See Returnables.

Mediated: The process by which library staff oversee the processing of ILL requests.

Non-returnables: Photocopies, copies of microform, and other materials the owning library does not expect to have returned.

Photocopies: See Non-returnables.

Professional: Since the criteria for determining professional status vary among libraries, report the number of staff members you consider professional, including, when appropriate, staff without library degrees.

Returnables: Items the owning library expects to have returned (books, AV, microforms, etc.).

Students: Students and others employed on an hourly basis whose Hourly staff wages are paid from funds from the library budget or from another budget (e.g., federal work-study programs).

Support staff: Full-time library staff in clerical, para- or non-professional positions. May or may not have supervisory responsibilities.

Unmediated: The process by which patrons identify items, potential suppliers, and initiate ILL requests for those materials without the assistance of library staff.

III. Contact Information

Mary E. Jackson is the Principal Investigator for the ILL/DD Performance Measures Study. Please direct all questions to her. She will respond as quickly as possible. Please mail complete instruments to the address noted below.

email: mary@arl.org
phone: 202/296-2296
fax: 202/872-0884
address: Association of Research Libraries
21 Dupont Circle Suite 800
Washington, DC 20036

IV. Deadline

The deadline for completion of the Cost Component is **September 30, 1996.**

PART II: QUESTIONNAIRE: ILL Cost Data

I. General Instructions

1 Please read all instructions carefully before answering the questionnaire. This questionnaire collects data comparable to the original cost study. However, the format and specific questions have been revised and updated. Use the enclosed worksheets for data entry.

2 Fill in your institutional name on all worksheets. Complete all questions. If the appropriate answer is zero or none, use "0." If the appropriate answer is not applicable, use "NA." If an exact figure is not available, estimate the total by collecting a two-week sample and annualizing the total or providing an estimate. Use the "Comments" section to expand on or clarify your responses.

3 Report data for the central ILL unit, or, in the case of decentralized ILL operations, for the main library or largest ILL service unit. Please be sure to indicate the name of the unit.

4 Supply data for the entire fiscal year. Report actual statistics collected, or collect a two-week sample and annualize. When figures are not available, use the most recent cost figures and statistics available for the category. Indicate annualized data with an asterisk (*).

5 Supply accurate data. If information available for a particular category is for the library as a whole, estimate the ILL percentage by collecting a two-week sample and annualizing, or consulting staff most closely involved in the activity. Without accurate data, incomplete or inaccurate conclusions may be drawn.

6 Separate borrowing and lending costs, and within each as requested, track returnable and non-returnable costs. If you cannot answer the questions that ask specifically for returnables/non-returnable data, we will calculate the proportions from answers to question IV-1 in the General Questionnaire section.

II. WORKSHEET 1: Staff Costs

Overview: When identifying staff, include all staff who handle or process ILL transactions. Staff may work in the ILL unit as well as other library departments or branch libraries. The aim is to be comprehensive in accounting for all staff time spent in processing ILL requests.

For example, if ILL requests are accepted at a branch library or the central Reference desk, photocopying completed by a outside contract service, or packages wrapped by mailroom staff, a portion of the staff time in each of those units and operations should be counted.

See the Definitions Section for explanations of the various categories of staff.

The Worksheet includes an example of a staff member who works four (4) days a week for the library, thus 80% of the normal 35 hour workweek. The individual is a support staff, has an annual salary of $18,720, with a fringe of $3,931 (21%). The fringe is paid by the library. The total reimbursement is $22,651. The individual works 3 days in ILL, and 1 day in circulation, so the percentage in ILL is 75%. All of the time in ILL is spent on borrowing, thus the percentage borrowing is 100%, and 0% in lending.

A. STAFF: Identify all individuals who assist in the processing of ILL requests and complete a separate row on the worksheet for each. Separate staff assigned to the ILL unit from those who perform ILL tasks but are primarily responsible for other library duties. Use any name, initials, or code that would permit subsequent verification of data.

B. % FTE: Use a number between 1 and 100 to indicate the amount of the institution's normal workweek the individual works. Answer should be no greater than 100.

C. TYPE: Indicate position type using definitions at bottom of the worksheet.

D. ANNUAL SALARY: For each staff, record the annual salary. Convert part-time, hourly, or monthly salaries to an annual rate. Use the salary for the incumbent. Do not use the average for the classification or ranking of the individual. ARL guarantees confidentiality of individual salaries and will not include an institution's data if individual salaries can be inferred.

E. FRINGE AMOUNT: Record the institutional fringe (staff) benefit amount in dollars for all individuals who receive fringe benefits. Convert a percentage rate to an annual fringe compensation. Include the amount even if paid by the parent institution or outside organization.

F. FRI. PAID BY: Indicate the department or organization paying fringe benefits using the definitions at the bottom of the worksheet.

G. TOTAL REIMBURSEMENT: Record the total of C, Annual Salary, and D, Fringe Amount.

H. % WORKED IN ILL: Of the total amount of time worked (indicated in B), calculate the % of time for each staff working on ILL requests. See notes 1 and 2 below for instructions on how to calculate the percentage.

I. % BORROWING: Of the percentage worked in ILL, determine the percentage of time each staff spends on processing ILL borrowing transactions. If possible, count returnables and non-returnables. If the total amount or percentage for borrowing is not known, keep a detailed log of time spent on ILL activities for two weeks or use the percentages from the formal job descriptions.

The percentage of I and J must total 100%. However, this sum is the total of the time the individual works on ILL requests.

J. % LENDING: Determine the percentage of time each staff spends on processing ILL lending transactions. If possible, count returnables and non-returnables. If the total amount or percentage for lending is not known, keep a detailed log of time spent on ILL activities for two weeks and annualize or use the percentages from formal job descriptions.

Additional Instructions for Staff:

1 Time away from the ILL Unit. Many staff assigned to work in the ILL unit full-time will spend some portion of their work week attending meetings, training sessions, or performing other non-ILL related library functions. This time away from processing ILL requests should not be deducted from the time assigned for ILL tasks. Count staff who work in ILL full-time as 100% ILL, even if they attend meetings, etc.

2 Staff with multiple responsibilities. Some staff in the ILL unit have non-ILL responsibilities assigned on a regular basis. For example, if an individual is assigned to work in ILL 60% of the week and 40% in circulation, record 60% in Column G, % Worked in ILL. Of that 60%, the time spent on borrowing and lending must total 100%.

3 Part-time employees. Some employees work fewer hours than the institutionally- defined full-time work week. For example, an individual may work 20 hours a week for the library, all in ILL. Convert that 20 hour-a-week salary into an annual salary.

4 Student employees. Report the wages paid for the fiscal year. Include students on financial aid, even though the library does not directly pay their wages.

5 Vacant positions. If the ILL unit has a vacant position during the data collection period but expects to fill the position, record the annual salary of the previous incumbent, calculate the annual salary of the most recent incumbent, or report the annual salary expected to be offered to the new employee.

6 Outside reimbursement. Include staff for whom the library gets partial or full reimbursement from a source other than the library, or for whom there is no cost (e.g. temporary replacements hired from an employment agency). Use the annual salary equivalent for those staff. If staff are paid by an outside agency, use the salary & benefits paid by the library or institution to the agency, rather than the amount paid by the agency to the individual.

III. WORKSHEET 2: Network and Communication Costs

A. NETWORK/COMMUNICATION: For each method used to send and receive ILL requests, calculate costs using the details as examples. Use annual or monthly invoices to determine total costs.

B. TOTAL: Record total costs for each category.

C. % BORROWING: Calculate the proportion of use for borrowing. If necessary, keep a two week log to determine the percentage.

D. % LENDING: Calculate the proportion of use for borrowing. If necessary, keep a two week log to determine the percentage.

Additional Instructions for Network/Communication:

1 Types. Include applicable telephone, Ariel, electronic mail, Internet, and network fees (OCLC, RLIN, etc.).

2 Telephone. Calculate total cost for borrowing and lending, or estimate percentage for borrowing and lending. If actual costs are not known, keep a two-week log including the following:

Local service costs. The flat rate phone fees, local area message unit costs. Include only desk phones. Charges for other telecommunication equipment (fax & email are captured elsewhere in the survey).

Long distance. Long distance charges for calls made to support either borrowing or lending.

3 Membership fees. Do not include membership fees unless the network is used exclusively by or for ILL.

4 Actual costs. Actual costs are highly desirable, but if cost of electronic mail and network and services are unavailable, use vendor price lists.

5 Exclude fax. Do not include fax telecommunication costs in this section; include fax costs on Worksheet 3: Delivery.

IV. WORKSHEET 3: Delivery Costs

A. BORROWING: Include the cost of mailing articles to patrons; mailing or faxing ALA ILL request forms to potential lenders; pick-up notices, overdues, and recalls to patrons; returning borrowed items to the owning library, and other materials related to borrowing.

B. LENDING: Include the cost of shipping returnables and non-returnables to the requesting library or individual, overdues and recalls, returning unfilled ALA request forms, and other materials related to lending.

Additional Instructions for Delivery Costs:

1 If postage and other delivery costs for ILL transactions cannot be separated from general library delivery expenses, determine the percentage applicable to ILL through actual records or keep a two-week log.

2 FAX charges. Determine fax charges from actual phone bills or a two-week log. If the fax machine is rented, include the local and long distance charges in this section, and the rental expenses on Worksheet 6, Equipment and Maintenance. Separate borrowing and lending charges if possible.

3 Ariel charges. Include costs for Ariel transmission of ILL request forms as a borrower and articles as a lender, etc.

4 Commercial delivery services. Include costs incurred for Federal Express, UPS, Purolator, Pony Express, other commercial parcel couriers.

5 Courier services. Include costs incurred using inter-institutional shuttle services, state-wide delivery services, or other delivery service or carriers between institutions.

6 Non-ILL shipments. If the delivery service is used for purposes other than just interlibrary loan, include the ILL portion of the cost, or keep a two-week log. If staff costs can be separated out, include those costs in Worksheet 1. Otherwise, include here all costs associated with the ILL delivery service—staff, vehicles (using 25% of purchase cost if vehicle is less than four years old), and maintenance, etc. Separate borrowing and lending charges, if possible.

7 Multiple shipments. If a package contains both borrowing and lending material, try to determine the majority of the material and include in that category. If exact proportions cannot be determined, separate based on annual borrowing and lending proportions. If a package contains both returnables and non-returnables, count as a returnable.

V. WORKSHEET 4: Photocopy Costs

A. BORROWING: Record total costs of photocopying the patron's citation or source of information; borrowing policy sheets; letters/overdues to patrons; copying invoices to be paid, borrowing policy statements; and all other in-house copying of forms for borrowing.

B. LENDING: Record total costs of all photocopies made in response to individual photocopy orders from other libraries or individuals; lending policy sheets; overdue notices, invoices, recalls, and other in-house copying for lending. Separate into returnables and non-returnables, if possible.

Additional Instructions for Photocopy Costs:

1 Type of copying. Include all types of copying: paper-to-paper, microform-to-microform, microform-to-paper. Do not include paper-to-microform copies.

2 Copying by non-ILL staff. Many libraries assign responsibility for ILL photocopying to non-ILL staff or units. Copying may be done by a central photocopy service, by a service managed by an outside organization, or by branch/departmental library staff. The costs for those staff should be included in Worksheet 1, Staff.

3 Related costs. Whenever possible, include costs of equipment, etc. associated with the photocopy activity under the relevant categories (Staff, Equipment, etc.).

4 Article length & page charges. When actual ILL photocopy costs are not available, estimate the total

number of pages photocopied for lending each year and apply your institutional article length and per page charge. If your per page costs include staff and equipment, do not include those costs in those categories. Use the following formula if you cannot determine institutional article length or page charges.

7 pages per article $0.07 per page

VI. WORKSHEET 5: Supply Costs

A. BORROWING: Record total costs for specialized supplies used primarily for borrowing. Include printer, fax, or photocopy paper; printer ribbons or ink cartridges; patron request forms; mailing labels; ALA Interlibrary Loan request forms; imprinted forms or envelopes; book bands; policy statements and handouts; flyers and brochures; book trucks; padded bags and other mailing supplies; and other supplies for borrowing. Pro-rate between borrowing and lending if necessary.

B. LENDING: Record total costs for specialized supplies used primarily for lending. Include printer, fax, or photocopy paper; printer ribbons or ink cartridges; mailing labels; imprinted forms or envelopes; book bands; policy statement and handouts; flyers and brochures; padded bags and other mailing supplies; and other supplies for lending. Pro-rate between lending and borrowing if necessary.

Additional Instructions for Supply Costs:

1 Office supplies. Cost for general office supplies such as pencils and paper clips are minimal and should not be included in supply costs. Do not count paper if counted in the Photocopies Section.

VII. WORKSHEET 6: Equipment, Software and Maintenance Costs

A. ITEM: Include all equipment and software used in ILL such as PCs, OCLC & RLIN workstations, Ariel workstations and software, fax machines, word processing or database software, OPAC terminals, SAVE-IT or AVISO management software, etc.

B: AGE: Record the age of the equipment and software using the definitions at the bottom of the worksheet. If age is unknown, use 4+ years old. Use this column to record donated equipment.

C. PURCHASE PRICE: Determine the purchase price of each item using invoices and price lists. This model assumes an average "life" for equipment or software to be four years. Record the purchase price if the equipment or software is 4 years old or less. Equipment older than four years should be listed with a purchase price of $0.00. Use "UA" if age is unknown.

D. RECURRING COSTS: Determine the annual maintenance fee, rental, software licensing fee, or other recurring costs for each piece of equipment. Include costs that have not already been included in other cost categories (such as Network).

E. TOTAL COST: Total C, 25% of Purchase Price, and D, Recurring Costs, and record in this column.

F. % BORROWING: Determine the percentage of use based on cost for borrowing activities. If possible, separate into returnables and non-returnables.

G. % LENDING: Determine the percentage of use for lending activities. If possible, separate into returnables and non-returnables.

Additional Instructions for Equipment/Software/ Maintenance Costs:

1 This model employs the concept of annual use charges, widely used in government contracts, to assign an estimated cost for equipment even in periods when no new equipment is purchased.

2 Shared equipment. If the equipment is used by ILL and other departments, calculate/estimate the percentage of use by ILL staff. Calculate the borrowing and lending use from that percentage. Use the section on shared staff to assist in calculating use of shared equipment.

VIII. WORKSHEET 7: Borrower Fees

A. TYPE OF FEE: The worksheet lists common fees paid to obtain materials from other libraries, document suppliers, and other sources. Itemize under "Other" any fees not included in this list. If borrower fees cannot be itemized by returnable or non-returnable, record the total in Column D.

B. RETURNABLES: Include amount expended from deposit accounts, prepaid coupons, international reply coupons, postage reimbursement, invoices paid, and other charges incurred in borrowing materials for your patrons.

C. NON-RETURNABLES: Include deposit accounts, prepaid coupons, international postal coupons, IFLA coupons, invoices paid, fees paid to suppliers (including libraries and document delivery suppliers), Copyright Clearance Center charges, royalty fees paid directly to copyright holders, and other fees paid to obtain photocopies for your patrons.

D. TOTAL: If a breakdown by returnables and non-returnables is not possible, list the total fees for each type.

IX. WORKSHEET 8: Reimbursements

A. TYPE OF INCOME: The worksheet lists common types of income for both borrowing and lending activities. Itemize under "Other" any income not included in this list.

B. BORROWING–RETURNABLES: Include lending and processing/rush delivery fees reimbursed by your patrons. Include fees charged when requests are submitted, reimbursement by state or consortial organizations, reimbursement for any of the cost categories (staffing, networks, delivery, etc.) received from an outside organization, and any other reimbursement for returnables.

C. BORROWING–NON-RETURNABLES: Include supply and processing/rush delivery fees reimbursed by

your patrons. Include fees charged when requests are submitted, reimbursement by state or consortial organizations, reimbursement for any of the cost categories (staffing, networks, delivery, etc.) received from an outside organization, and any other reimbursement for returnables.

D. BORROWING–TOTAL: Total Columns B and C, or list the total income for each type if income cannot be broken down between returnables and non-returnables.

E. LENDING–RETURNABLES: Include loan fees, processing/rush delivery surcharges, searching fees, postage/delivery charges, net lender reimbursement fees, reimbursements from the state or other organizations, or reimbursement for any of the cost categories (staffing, networks, delivery, etc.) received from an outside organization, and any other reimbursement for returnables.

F. LENDING–NON-RETURNABLES: Include photocopy fees, fax surcharges, delivery fees, searching fees, postage/delivery fees, lost book charges, net lender reimbursement fees, reimbursements from the state or other organizations, or reimbursement for any of the cost categories (staffing, networks, delivery, etc.) received from a library or individual, and any other reimbursement for non-returnables.

G. LENDING–TOTAL: Total Columns E and F, or list the total income for each type if income cannot be broken down between returnables and non-returnables.

APPENDIX H: GENERAL CHARACTERISTICS QUESTIONNAIRE

ARL Interlibrary Loan/Document Delivery
Performance Measures Study
General Characteristics of the ILL Unit
August, 1996

The following questions are designed to elicit general information about the characteristics and services of the ILL unit for which the cost data are being collected. Responses will be used with the other performance measures collected.

I. General Institutional Profile

1 Reporting Institution:

2 Name/location of ILL operation:

3 Person completing survey:

4 Position:

5 Phone: FAX: email:

6 Contact person (if different):

7 Phone: FAX: email:

8 Date survey returned to ARL:

9 Data collected is requested for the fiscal year July, 1995 to June, 1996. If different, please indicate the period for which you are supplying data:

    Reporting period: _____

II. Organizational/Administrative Questions:

1 Total number of separate ILL processing units in library system (a processing unit is one that has responsibility for borrowing, lending, or both): _____

2 Number of branch/departmental libraries served by the central ILL processing unit: _____

3 How would you characterize your services for the main ILL processing unit?

	Borrowing	Lending
Centralized	_____	_____
Decentralized	_____	_____

4 Organizationally, in which department/division is ILL included?

Public Services	_____
Access Services	_____
Reference	_____
Circulation	_____
Acquisitions	_____
Technical services	_____
Other (please specify)	_____

5 Who has day-to-day responsibility for the ILL operation? (Check one)

Administrative head	_____
Support staff supervisor	_____
Other (please specify):	_____

6 Indicate how borrowing and lending functions are administratively organized. (For example, check separate if borrowing is part of Reference and lending is part of Circulation.)

Combined _____   Separate borrowing & lending _____

7 For the libraries that completed the 1992 ARL/RLG ILL Cost Study, has the ILL operation undergone any major changes that would impact on unit costs since the original study? If so, summarize the changes. Examples of changes might include adding staffing or changing levels, upgrading equipment for all staff, significantly increasing use of document delivery suppliers.

Yes _____   No _____

III. Staffing Questions:

1 How many hours in a normal work week does an individual library staff member work (e.g. does FTE equal 40 hours?)?

35	_____
37.5	_____
40	_____
other (please specify)	_____

2 Is the library staff unionized?

	Yes	No
Professional	_____	_____
Support Staff	_____	_____

3 Does the professional staff have faculty status?

Yes _____   No _____

4 Staffing level

List the number of staff (FTE) in the central ILL processing unit. (See the Definitions Section for clarification of these terms.)

	Borrowing	Lending
Administrative Head		
Support staff supervisor		
Professional non-supervisor		
Support staff		
Students/hourly staff		
Volunteers		
Other (please specify)		

5 Check the tasks performed by ILL staff. (Check all that apply.)

BORROWING

_____ receiving requests from patrons/ responding to patrons

_____ searching local holdings

_____ verification/location searching

_____ initiating requests

_____ maintaining requests on OCLC, RLIN, etc.

_____ receiving/unwrapping material

_____ processing material for patrons

_____ charging/discharging materials on circ module of OPAC

_____ overdues/recalls/renewals

_____ invoicing/billing patrons

_____ collecting fines

_____ wrapping/returning materials

_____ filing/recordkeeping

_____ statistics

_____ general supervision and planning

_____ other (please specify)

LENDING

_____ receiving requests from other libraries

_____ searching for call numbers/local availability

_____ retrieving material from stacks

_____ photocopying

_____ faxing/Arieling

_____ wrapping/shipping/unwrapping

_____ checking out material on local circ system

_____ invoicing/billing/depositing checks

_____ overdues/recalls

_____ reshelving

_____ collecting fines

_____ filing

_____ statistics

_____ other

IV. Questions about Level and Type of Activity

1 Borrowing Activity

	Filled	Unfilled	Total
Total requests			
Returnables			
Non-returnables			

2 Borrowing Activity—Level of Difficulty

Record the level of difficulty of verifying requests received from your patrons.

Very easy to verify	_____
Fairly easy to verify	_____
Average difficulty	_____
Fairly difficult to verify	_____
Very difficult to verify	_____

3 Lending Activity

	Filled	Unfilled	Total
Total requests			
Returnables	_____	_____	_____
Non-returnables	_____	_____	_____

4 Lending Activity—Level of Difficulty

Record the level of difficulty of verifying/locating requests received from other libraries.

Very easy to verify	_____
Fairly easy to verify	_____
Average difficulty	_____
Fairly difficult to verify	_____
Very difficult to verify	_____

V. Questions about Equipment & Services

1 Transmission Methods

Provide or estimate the percentage of use for each of the methods by which ILL requests can be received by or sent to another library. Each column must total 100%. (Do not include the transmission methods used by patrons to submit ILL requests.)

	Borrowing	Lending
OCLC	_____	_____
RLIN	_____	_____
WLN	_____	_____
Docline	_____	_____
E-mail/Internet	_____	_____
OPAC ILL module	_____	_____
Mail/Post	_____	_____
Ariel	_____	_____
Supplier dedicated system (UnCover, etc.)	_____	_____
Fax	_____	_____
Other	_____	_____
TOTAL	100%	100%

2 Does your library engage in international ILL?

Yes _____ Borrowing only _____

No _____ Lending only _____

If yes, prioritize the areas/countries used for borrowing and lending. Use #1 for most frequently used, #6 for least used. Provide the number of requests for #1, the most frequently used country/area.

	Borrowing	Lending
Canada	_____	_____
Europe	_____	_____
Asia	_____	_____
Australia	_____	_____
Africa	_____	_____
Central/S. America	_____	_____
U.S.	_____	_____

3 Indicate if any of the following OCLC services are used:

	Yes	No
ILL Fee Management	_____	_____
Custom Holdings	_____	_____
ILL Prism Transfer	_____	_____
First Search-Prism ILL link	_____	_____
MicroEnhancer	_____	_____
"Enter my symbol twice"	_____	_____
Check union lists	_____	_____

4 Do you have one workstation per full-time staff (workstation defined as a computer able to access the local catalog, national utilities, Internet, local management software, etc.)?

Yes _____ No _____

5 Check all equipment & software located in the ILL office or used primarily by ILL staff. Double check those accessed by, but not located in the ILL office.

	Borrowing	Lending
Ariel	_____	_____
AVISO software	_____	_____
DOCLINE workstation(s)	_____	_____
Fax	_____	_____
Multiple access workstation(s)	_____	_____
Online Catalog terminal(s)	_____	_____
Photocopy machine(s)	_____	_____
RLIN workstation(s)	_____	_____
Save-It software	_____	_____
WLN workstation(s)	_____	_____
Other (please specify)	_____	_____

6 Check the delivery methods used.

	Borrowing	Lending
Ariel	_____	_____
Fax	_____	_____
Federal Express	_____	_____
Internet	_____	_____
Pony Express	_____	_____
Postal service	_____	_____
Relais	_____	_____
State-regional courier(s)	_____	_____
UPS	_____	_____
Other (please specify)	_____	_____

VI. Borrowing

1 Do you limit the number of requests your patrons can submit per day/week/month/term? Check yes if limits of any type have been established for any type of patron category.

Yes _____   No _____

2 Can your patrons submit requests electronically? Check Yes if you offer Prism ILL link, email, gopher or Web ILL request form, etc.

Yes _____   No _____

3 Do you charge your patrons for (check yes, if you charge any type of patron)

	Yes	No	Depends
Returnables?	_____	_____	_____
Non-returnables?	_____	_____	_____

4 Does your library use document delivery suppliers to fill photocopy requests? If so, estimate the percentage of photocopy requests filled by document suppliers.

Yes _____   No _____   % of total filled _____

5 Where do your patrons submit requests? Check all that apply.

ILL office	_____
Reference desk	_____
Circulation desk	_____
Branch/dept. library	_____
Electronically	_____
Other (please specify)	_____

6 Where do your patrons pick up ILL materials? Check all that apply.

	Returnables	Non-returnables
ILL office	_____	_____
Reference desk	_____	_____
Circulation desk	_____	_____
Branch/dept. library	_____	_____
Material mailed to patron	_____	_____
Other (please specify)	_____	_____

7 Check all patron categories for which you borrow.

Undergraduate	_____
Graduate student	_____
Faculty	_____
Staff (including library)	_____
Courtesy/community	_____
Other (please specify)	_____

8 Does the library have a separate budget line for borrowing expenses? (For example, does the library budget track ILL expenditures and/or income for such items as lending fees, CCC, delivery, fees collected from patrons?)

Yes _____ No _____

9 List the number of reciprocal agreements for the following types.

	Returnables	Non-returnables
Individual library	_____	_____
Regional Consortia	_____	_____
Statewide agreements	_____	_____
Networks (BCR, etc.)	_____	_____
Utilities (RLG, etc.)	_____	_____
Other (please specify)	_____	_____

10 Estimate the percentage of borrowing requests filled by libraries using reciprocal agreements in order to avoid processing and/or payment of lending fees. _____

VII. Lending

1 Do you charge institutions with whom you do not have cooperative and/or reciprocal arrangements?

Yes, charge for loan requests	_____
Yes, charge for photocopy requests	_____
No	_____

2 Check the payment methods you accept (for either loans or copies):

Charge (VISA, MC, AmEx, etc.) _____

Check _____

Coupon (any type) _____

Deposit account _____

Invoice _____

Other (please specify) _____

OCLC IFM _____

3 List the number of reciprocal agreements for the following types.

	Returnables	Non-returnables
Individual library		
Regional Consortia		
Statewide agreements		
Networks (AMIGOS, etc.)		
Utilities (RLG, etc.)		
Other (please specify)		

4 Does the lending operation retain the income generated for either returnables or non-returnables?

Yes _____   No _____

APPENDIX I: COST WORKSHEETS

WORKSHEET 1	Staff								
A	B	C	D	E	F	G	H	I	J
Staff	% FTE	Type	Annual Salary	Fringe Amt.	Fringe Paid By	Total Reimb.	% in ILL	% Borr.	% Lend.
EXAMPLE	80	4	$18,720	$3,931	1	$22,651	75	100	0
ILL Staff:									
Other Staff:									

TYPE:

1= Professional Supervisor   4= Support Staff

2= Professional Non-Supervisor   5= Student Asst.

3= Support Staff Supervisor   6= Volunteer

FRINGE PAID BY:

1= Library   3= State

2= Instit.   4= Other

WORKSHEET 2	Network and Communication		
A	B	C	D
Network/Communication	Total	% Borrowing	% Lending
Phone			
Local			
Long-distance			
OCLC			
ILL display holdings			
UL holdings display ILL			
Prism scan title–ILL			
Prism keyword search–ILL			
ILL loan basic			
ILL loan review (Prism)			
ILL stat rpt per page			
Shpg ILL stats rpt			
IFM administration fee			
Search ILL subtotals			
IPT			
General member fee			
OCLC full user fee			
Regional network admin. fee			
Documentation/users guide			
EPIC searching			
Other			

WORKSHEET 2	Network and Communication (p. 2)		
A	**B**	**C**	**D**
Network/Communication	Total	% Borrowing	% Lending
RLIN			
Dialup			
Telecommunications			
Connect hr. chg, search only			
Dedicated IP network link fee			
Dedicated IP network port fee			
Dedicated IP network host fee			
Private async link fee			
Private async port fee			
Private async host fee			
Reserve dial link fee			
Reserve dial port fee			
Reserve dial host fee			
Network dial port fee			
Internet host port fee			
PC maintenance			
Account activity			
Acct activity x per search rate			
% of fixed price contract approp. to ILL			
Other			

WORKSHEET 2	Network and Communication (p. 3)		
A	**B**	**C**	**D**
Network/Communication	Total	% Borrowing	% Lending
WLN			
ILL request			
ILL, BIB, IPOLICY commands			
Database searches (based on ILL use)			
Simultaneous sessions (based on % ILL use)			
Hourly connect charge (based on % ILL use)			
Internet			
Dedicated line			
Downloading			
Set-up			
Training			
Documentation			
Other			
REFCATSS			
Hourly network access charges			
Network access			
Unreg. terminal			
Hourly per terminal			
Flat-rate network access charges			
Network access			
Registered term.			
Searching fees			
Searching			
Other access points			
ILL transactions			
Interlibrary loans			
ILL - trans.			
Other			

WORKSHEET 2 — Network and Communication (p. 4)

A	B	C	D
Network/Communication	Total	% Borrowing	% Lending
AMICUS			
Online connection			
Datapac			
Internet			
Dedicated line			
Downloading			
Set-up			
Training/documentation			
ALL OTHER NETWORKS			
Ethernet access			
Membership fee (If ILL exclusive)			
Transaction fees			
Other charges/fees			

WORKSHEET 3 — Delivery

	A	B
	Borrowing Expenditures	Lending Expenditures
Postal service		
FAX		
Ariel		
Commercial delivery services		
Courier services		
Other		

WORKSHEET 4 — Photocopy Costs

	A	B
	Borrowing Expenditures	Lending Expenditures
Photocopy costs		

WORKSHEET 5	Supplies		
		A	B
		Borrowing Expenditures	Lending Expenditures
Supplies			

WORKSHEET 6	Equipment/Software/Maintenance					
A	B	C	D	E	F	G
Item	Age	Purchase price	Recurring costs	Total cost	% Borrowing	% Lending

AGE:

1 = 0-1 year   3 = 4+ years

2 = 1-4 years   4 = donated

WORKSHEET 7	Borrower Fees		
A	B	C	D
Type of Fee	Returnables	Non-returnables	Total
Deposit accounts			
Coupons			
Invoices/direct charges			
OCLC IFM debit			
Net borrower charges			
Document delivery suppliers			
Copyright Clearance Center			
Copyright royalty payments			
Other			

WORKSHEET 8	Reimbursements					
A	B	C	D	E	F	G
Type of Income	Borr Ret	Borr Non-ret	Borr Total	Lend Ret	Lend Non-ret	Lend Total
Fees from local patrons						
Per-transaction reimb.						
State reimb.						
Consortial reimb.						
National/other lib. reimb.						
Coupon sales						
Deposit account income						
Reimb. for staff						
Reimb. for network/ consortia						
OCLC lending credit						
OCLC IFM lib to lib credit						
RLG Shares lending credit						
WLN ILL loan credit						
Reimb. for delivery						
Reimb. for equip/ software						
Reimb. for supplies						
Other						

APPENDIX J: TURNAROUND TIME AND USER SATISFACTION INSTRUCTIONS AND WORKSHEET

TO: ILL/DD Performance Measures Study Participants

FROM: Mary E. Jackson, Access & Delivery Services Consultant

DATE: 21 October 1996

RE: Phase Two Data Collection

Over 110 ARL and Oberlin Group institutions are participating in the ILL/DD Performance Measures Study. ARL participants are beginning to return their completed instruments for Phase One. Oberlin Group participants are on a slightly later timetable. Both groups, however, are receiving Part Two instruments with this mailing.

Phase Two of the Performance Measures Study collects data on turnaround time, fill rate, and user satisfaction by using a sampling technique. Over the next five (5) to six (6) weeks, between 125 - 150 new borrowing requests will be randomly selected and tracked.

We are aware that a few of the study participants are significant net lenders, and as a result, may receive fewer than 150 new borrowing requests during the data collection period. Please contact me if you are concerned that your volume of incoming borrowing activity may not be sufficiently high for you to participate in this phase of the study.

Included are the following:

1 General Instructions

2 Data collection form for turnaround time and fill rate & User Satisfaction Questionnaire

3 Log sheet for tracking outstanding requests

Your institutional ID number will be used to track Phase Two requests. Your institutional ID number is

_____ .

A reminder to ARL participants: If you haven't already returned the Phase One forms, I encourage you to send me an email (mary@arl.org) to let me know when you expect to return Phase One worksheets.

ARL ILL/DD PERFORMANCE MEASURES STUDY: PHASE TWO

General Instructions

1 Overview & Summary

Between 125 and 150 new borrowing requests will be sampled to measure turnaround time, fill rate, and user satisfaction. We will use this sample to project turnaround time and fill rate for your institution and to calculate aggregate totals for all participants.

We are using the same sample for all three measures, in part to determine if there is a correlation between turnaround time and user satisfaction on a request-by-request basis.

2 General Definitions

Phase Two of the study focuses on borrowing operations. We define turnaround time, fill rate, and user satisfaction from the perspective of the borrowing library. For the purpose of this study, the following definitions are used:

Turnaround time is the number of calendar days between the patron's initiation of an ILL/DD request and the library's notification to the patron of the final outcome of the request. It is typically divided into three stages:

1 initial processing time, including verification, location identification, and initiation of the first ILL transaction;

2 time to obtain document, including supplier's processing time, delivery time, and the borrower's resubmission of unfilled requests to other suppliers; and

3 post-receipt processing, includes the receipt of the document or the final negative response, material processing, and notification of the patron.

Fill rate is the number of successfully filled ILL/DD requests as a percentage of the total number of borrowing requests submitted. Our sample of 150 requests can be used as an example to determine fill rate. If 150 borrowing requests were submitted and 131 were filled, the fill rate is 87%.

User satisfaction is the extent to which the needs of a specific user are met. For the purpose of this study, user satisfaction is correlated with specific ILL requests rather than their overall satisfaction or dissatisfaction with the general interlibrary loan and document delivery process.

3 Time Frame & Selection Process

In each of the next five (5) to six (6) weeks, randomly select five (5) requests per workday, for a total of twenty-five (25) requests per week, or 125 to 150 requests total. It is not necessary to begin the selection process at the beginning of a work week. It is not necessary to choose requests from five different individuals, however, it may be desirable to track requests from different patrons.

Two methods for random selection are offered; similar methods may also be used.

1 Select every X request at the point at which you begin processing new borrowing requests (for example, each morning). That number will vary depending on the number of new requests you are receiving each day.

2 Select any five requests if requests are counted and processed throughout the workday.

4 Sample Size

Although we are asking you to track at least 125 requests, we would like to receive a minimum of 100 returned transaction forms per institution. Feel free to select more than 5 requests per day in order to ensure a return of at least 100.

5 Prepare Worksheets

A copy of the worksheet is included in this mailing. Record your institutional ID on the master. Photocopy 150 copies, or more if you will be selecting more than five requests per day. Sequentially number each form with a transaction number from 1 to 150, or higher as needed.

6 Identify Sample Requests

It is important to mark the sample requests in a manner that will make tracking requests simple for all staff. Use any method that will work for your own operation. Suggestions include:

- highlight the top of form with a brightly colored marker,

- annotate form with "ARL study" or similar phrase, or

- enclose the work card in a brightly colored plastic sleeve.

Attach workforms securely to patrons' forms so staff can easily update requests as they work their way through the process.

7 Track Sample Requests

Each time a marked sample request enters a new phase of the process, annotate the worksheet with the appropriate date. The sample reflects a filled, but simple ILL/DD request for a photocopy of a journal article (a non-returnable).

8 Distribute the User Satisfaction Survey

The worksheet has been designed to detach the user satisfaction questionnaire for distribution to the patron. The method by which you will distribute the form to the user will depend on your internal procedures.

If you mail photocopies or books to your patrons, staple or attached the user questionnaire with the item.

If patrons pick up materials, include the user questionnaire in the material in a place visible to both staff and users. Feel free to encourage staff to encourage cooperation from the users to participate in the study.

Patron questionnaires should be mailed to ARL at the address noted on the reverse of the form.

9 Return the Completed Worksheets

Please return completed worksheets in batches of 25 or more. Ensure that each includes your institution code and internal transaction number. Return the worksheets to Mary Jackson at the ARL office. Given the number we will handle, please use the postal service or commercial carrier (UPS, FedEx, etc.). There is no need to fax the workforms to us.

ARL ILL/DD Performance Measures Study
Phase Two Data Collection Form

1. Institution ID: 1234   2. Transaction #   45

3. TYPE OF REQUEST:

      Returnable   _____

      Non-returnable   XXX

4. DATE:

      a. Recorded on patron's request form   10-15-96

      b. Accepted at initial service point   10-16-96

      c. Processed by ILL staff   10-17-96

      d. Sent to first potential supplier   10-22-96

      e. Material received in ILL department   10-28-96

      f. Transaction not filled   _____

      g. Patron notified   10-28-96

5. FINAL OUTCOME OF REQUEST:

      Filled   XXX   Not filled   _____   Still in-process   _____

---

10 Complete Phase Two Tracking

We will notify you on the listserv of the date by which all outstanding requests should be returned. Because it is important to receive accurate information on all sample requests, tracking of outstanding requests will last at least eight (8) weeks. The enclosed log sheet may be useful in tracking and locating outstanding requests.

11 Understand the Worksheet Terminology

The following terms are used on the Phase Two worksheet.

1 Institution ID

The institutional ID number assigned to your library is included on the cover memo. Write or type your ID number on the line for Question 1: Institution ID on both sections of the worksheet. Photocopy at least 150 copies of the worksheet.

2 Transaction Number

This request-specific transaction number will be used to correlate data on fill rate and turnaround time with the results of the user satisfaction surveys. Sequentially number the worksheets from 1 to 150. Be sure to record the transaction number in both sections.

3 Type of Request

Returnable. A request for the loan of a book, AV, microform or other material you expect to return.

Non-returnable. A request for a photocopy of a journal article, copy of a reel of microfilm, or other copy you do not expect to return to the supplier.

Record the type of request at the beginning of the process, but change the type if the supplier changes the type. For example, if you asked for a copy of a paper in a conference proceedings you would check "non-returnable." However, if the supplier sent the proceedings on a loan, change the response in question 3 to "returnable." It is advisable to use a pencil for this section.

4 Dates

a *DATE RECORDED ON PATRON'S REQUEST FORM*

Date the patron records on the request form. For electronic patron request systems, use the system-supplied date.

b *ACCEPTED AT INITIAL SERVICE POINT*

Date accepted at the ILL office, reference or circulation desk, departmental or branch library, or in a tray or bin at a service point, etc.

Date may be same as 4a, particularly when the patron completes a paper form and turns it in at a service point.

c *PROCESSED BY ILL STAFF*

Date ILL staff begin to process the request. Processing includes checking for local availability, verifying correctness of bibliographic data, finding potential suppliers, etc. Use the date processing starts, *not* the date processing is finished.

This date may be the same as 4a and/or 4b, especially for rush requests.

d *SENT TO FIRST POTENTIAL SUPPLIER*

Date request sent to first potential library or supplier. Transmission may be electronic (OCLC, RLIN, fax, etc.) or surface (postal, courier, etc.).

This date may be the same as 4a, 4b, and/or 4c, especially for rush requests.

e *MATERIAL RECEIVED IN ILL DEPARTMENT*

Date material received in ILL unit. Do *not* count the date material was received in the mailroom. If the material is held over in the ILL office for processing at a later date, use the actual date of arrival, not the date of processing. Enter a date only if the request was filled.

Date may be same as 4d, especially if the request is a "rush."

Dates 4e and 4f are mutually exclusive—complete one *or* the other, not both.

f *TRANSACTION NOT FILLED*

Date ILL staff consider the request to be completed because it was not filled. Reasons requests are not filled include (but are not limited to) the following:

- canceled by the patron,
- passed the patron's "needs by" date,
- exhausted all suppliers,
- bad or incomplete citation,
- exceeded patron's "maxcost."

Do *not* use this date if request is being returned to patron temporarily for additional information with the expectation that the patron will return the request to the ILL department for additional process.

Dates 4e and 4f are mutually exclusive—complete one or the other, not both.

g *PATRON NOTIFIED/MATERIAL SENT*

Date patron was emailed or phoned, or the date the message or document was placed in the ILL department's outgoing mail for delivery via campus mail, postal service, etc. Message includes notification of material availability ("material ready to be picked up") and notification that the request could not be filled.

Date may be same as 4e, especially for rush requests, and/or 4f.

5 Final Outcome of Request

Filled: The request was filled and the patron received the material or was notified of material availability. Count a request as a filled request if the material was received, but the patron did not pick up the item.

Not filled: The request was not filled and the patron did not receive the material requested. This also includes requests for which an ILL transaction was not initiated, such as material owned locally.

Still in-process: The request is still an active request and the borrowing library is attempting to obtain the item from potential libraries or document suppliers.

ARL ILL/DD Performance Measures Study
Phase Two Data Collection Form

1. Institution ID: _____   2. Transaction # _____

3. TYPE OF REQUEST:

       Returnable _____   Non-returnable _____

4. DATE:

       a. Recorded on patron's request form _____

       b. Accepted at initial service point _____

       c. Processed by ILL staff _____

       d. Sent to first potential supplier _____

       e. Material received in ILL department _____

       f. Transaction not filled _____

       g. Patron notified _____

5. FINAL OUTCOME OF REQUEST:

       Filled _____   Not filled _____   Still in-process _____

Institution ID: _____   Transaction # _____

ILL/DD Performance Measures Study
User Satisfaction Questionnaire

The Association of Research Libraries (ARL) is studying interlibrary loan (ILL) and document delivery (DD) services in research and college libraries. One component of the study is to measure your satisfaction with specific ILL/DD requests submitted during the fall 1996 term. We seek your cooperation in completing this brief survey. Please answer the questions for the material or response to which this is attached. Your response is anonymous, but the coding on the survey will correlate aggregate data on your institution, the turnaround time, and fill rate for all ILL requests. Please answer the following questions and mail your completed response to the address noted below.

1. Did the item (or negative response) arrive within an acceptable time frame, or by the date by which you indicated you needed the request?   Yes _____   No _____

       If no, why? _____

2. Was quality of the photocopy acceptable or were all volumes of the book title or microform reels supplied?

       Yes _____   No _____

       If no, what was missing? _____

3. If the request was not filled, do you believe the ILL staff did all they could to obtain the item?

       Yes _____   No _____

       If no, why not? _____

4. Did you have to pay for this request?   Yes _____   No _____

       If yes, how much? _____

       If no, how much would you be willing to pay for this request? _____

Please return to: ILL/DD Study, Association of Research Libraries
21 Dupont Circle N.W. Suite 800, Washington, DC 20036

APPENDIX K: KEY TERMS USED IN THE STUDY

ILL/DD Performance Measures Study
Final Individual Institution Analysis Report:
Interpreting the Results
August, 1997

The ILL/DD Performance Measures Study is a two-year project designed to study the performance of interlibrary loan and document delivery operations in research and college libraries. The purpose of the study is to collect data on ILL/DD performance and to identify and describe characteristics of effective ILL/DD operations. The study was funded by The Andrew W. Mellon Foundation and conducted by the Association of Research Libraries in collaboration with the Council on Library and Information Resources.

A total of 119 libraries participated in the study: 97 research libraries (11 of which are branch or departmental libraries), and 22 college libraries. Nearly two-thirds of the research libraries also participated in the 1992 ARL/RLG Interlibrary Loan Cost Study.

The ILL/DD Performance Measures Study collected data on four performance measures: cost, fill rate, turnaround time, and user satisfaction. Participants collected data on costs and fill rate for borrowing and lending operations and turnaround time and user satisfaction for borrowing operations. Cost and fill rate were calculated using data from the library's most recent fiscal year. A random sample of 125 to 150 borrowing requests was used to collect data on turnaround time and user satisfaction. Most participants tracked the sample requests during the Fall 1996 term; some collected data during the Spring 1997 term.

THE PERFORMANCE MEASURES

The report presents data from your library and compares it with aggregate data from 97 research libraries or 22 Oberlin Group college library participants. Data on the four performance measures were calculated from the following sources:

Costs: Calculated using data from Cost Worksheets 1-8 and based on participants most recent complete fiscal year, which, for many, was July, 1995 to June, 1996.

Fill rate: Calculated using data from the General Characteristics questionnaire questions IV.1 (Borrowing

Activity) and IV.4 (Lending Activity). Fill rate information was also collected in the random sample and the two data sets will be analyzed and an analysis of possible differences will be included in the final report of the study.

Turnaround time: Calculated from the random sample of filled borrowing requests.

User satisfaction: Calculated from the random sample of borrowing requests for which the surveys were returned.

KEY TERMS USED IN THE INDIVIDUAL INSTITUTIONAL ANALYSIS: FINAL REPORT

1 Terms Used in the Aggregate Survey Data Ranges

Mean: The average, calculated using data from either research or college libraries. Please note this is a change from the preliminary report in which aggregate data were reported for college and university libraries. Each mean represents the "mean of the means," that is, the average of all library means in each category, not the mean of all observations.

Median: The middle point, calculated using data from either research or college libraries. Again, this is a change from the preliminary report in which aggregate data were reported for college and university libraries.

10-90%: This report aggregates data on research or college libraries. To protect confidentiality, the report presents the range of measures between 10% and 90%. Two examples may aid in interpretation.

For research libraries, the borrowing unit cost for 90% of participants was $27.84 or less; for lending, 25% of the research libraries reported a unit cost of $6.25 or less. The overall borrowing turnaround time for 25% of the research libraries is 12.5 days or less; 90% of the research libraries obtained non-returnables for their patrons in 22.4 days or less.

For Oberlin Group participants, the borrowing unit cost for 90% of participants was $18.50 or less; for lending, 25% of the Oberlin Group libraries reported a unit cost of $5.32 or less. The overall borrowing turnaround time for 25% of the Oberlin Group libraries is 7.6 days or less; 90% of the Oberlin Group libraries obtained non-returnables for their patrons in 16.6 days or less.

2 Terms Used to Describe the Performance Measures

Transactions (Filled): The number of filled ILL transactions, including total, borrowing, and lending. Totals for returnables and non-returnables are reported for borrowing and lending.

Unit Cost: The cost to the institution of one filled borrowing or lending transaction. Unit costs include staff, network and communication, delivery, photocopy, supplies, equipment, and for borrowers, borrowing fees. Unit costs for each of these categories are detailed further on pages 5-7 of the report.

Fill Rate: The percentage of borrowing and lending requests successfully filled.

Turnaround Time: For borrowing only, the number of calendar days from the date the patron submitted the request to the date the patron was notified of the material availability (or non-availability). Data are presented for overall turnaround time, for returnables, non-returnables, and for the number of requests still active at the end of the sample period. Turnaround time is also presented by the number of transactions completed within four defined periods of time, again, broken down by returnables and non-returnables.

On the bottom of page 2, the column reporting the mean represents a cumulative turnaround time total. That is, for research and Oberlin Group libraries, 73% of all returnable requests were filled within 14 days.

However, do not read down the columns for median, 10%, 25%, 75%, and 90th percentile for requests within a period of time. The research library represented at the 10th percentile completed only 1% of its requests within 0-3 days while the library at the 90th percentile completed 16% in the same time period. Likewise for Oberlin Group libraries, the results are 2% and 25%, respectively. It is possible that one library may fall at the 10% percentile for the 0-3 day category, but rise to the 90% percentile for the 0-14 day category.

Page 3 presents yet another view of turnaround time, that of the delays between each of the measured steps of the process. Note that the "overall turnaround time" may not be the sum of the steps in the ILL process. Data reporting errors or omissions in which only two or three dates were recorded on a form were not used to determine the mean number of days for each step in the process. As a result, overall turnaround time is a better measure of the time taken for the total ILL process. However, individual dates that differ significantly from the mean or median can indicate steps in the ILL process in which a library's performance is excellent or poor.

Page 3 includes two important footnotes. The first describes the end of year service suspension, defined as the percentage of sample requests submitted before December 25, 1996 and filled after December 26, 1996. The second footnote records the first and last dates on which ILL requests were sampled.

From the random sample, libraries with fewer than 50 filled requests or more than 50% of requests "still in process" should be cautious of using these numbers. Proper sampling dictates that more requests should be examined to get a better estimate of the days of delivery for these libraries. In addition, libraries with a significant number of requests "still in process" should regard their estimate of days of delivery as an underestimate of the true mean number of days. A reasonable rule of thumb is that libraries with 10% of the total requests still in process should add 3 days to their mean days for delivery.

User Survey: For borrowing only, the percent of local users who responded to questions that asked if the item or report of non-availability arrived within an acceptable timeframe, if the quality of the copy was acceptable or all volumes of the request were supplied, and if they believed ILL staff did all they could to obtain the item. Users were also asked whether they had to pay for the request, and if so, the amount. If users did not pay, they were asked how much they would be willing to pay to have the request filled. The number of responses for each category is also listed.

Several libraries had a limited number of survey participants that responded to questions regarding amount paid or willingness to pay. Libraries should be cautious interpreting these numbers.

3 Terms Used to Detail Costs: Staff

Staff Costs: Unit cost of all staff involved in the ILL process. Staff costs are reported for borrowing and lending, and further separate into ILL staff and other staff in the library. ILL and other library staff are also reported by five position categories.

Several libraries failed to record the employee type for one or more employees. As a result, breakdowns by ILL staff and Other staff may not sum to the total. In addition, libraries with very few staff in the ILL department will have categories that are either zero or a number significantly above the mean. Libraries should not interpret these numbers as indicating anything about staffing. It may be more worthwhile for these libraries to compare their categories (ILL Staff and Other Staff) with other participants and ignore the sub category unit costs.

ILL Staff: Unit cost of staff assigned to the ILL department or unit with primary responsibility for processing of borrowing or lending requests.

Other Staff: Unit cost of other library staff responsible for a portion of the ILL processing, such as circulation, reference, administrative, or departmental library staff, etc.

4 Terms Used to Define Major Staff Categories

Professional Supervisor: Unit cost of the administrative head of the overall ILL operation and the one assigned policy-making and planning responsibilities.

Professional Non-supervisor: Unit cost of professionals as defined by the institution, and including where appropriate, staff without library degrees.

Support Staff Supervisor: Unit cost of support staff with supervisory responsibilities, including responsibilities for day-to-day borrowing or lending operations.

Support Staff: Unit cost of support staff, including full-time and part-time.

Student Assistants: Unit cost of student assistants and others employed on an hourly basis.

5 Terms Used to Define Other Costs

Network & Communication Costs: Unit cost of telephone, OCLC, RLIN, other ILL network costs, Ethernet access, etc.

Delivery Costs: Unit cost of postal service, fax, Ariel, local or regional courier, commercial delivery services such as UPS or FedEx, etc.

Photocopy Costs: Unit cost of photocopying, including filling requests for other libraries, internal forms, patron citations, overdues, etc.

Supply Costs: Unit cost of paper, forms, mailing labels, ILL request forms, imprinted stationery, book bands, etc.

Equipment/Software/Maintenance Costs: Unit cost of personal computers, OCLC and RLIN workstations, Ariel workstations, fax machines, word processing and database software, ILL management software, etc.

Borrower Fees: Unit cost of fees paid to obtain materials from other libraries, document suppliers, and other sources, including deposit accounts, prepaid coupons, international reply coupons, postage reimbursement, etc. Includes transaction-specific borrowing fees only and not general membership fees.

Reimbursements: Unit cost of fees collected from local patrons (borrowing) and/or from other libraries (lending). Please note that unit costs do not include the reimbursements received. Therefore, unit costs reflect gross costs, not net costs.

APPENDIX L: A NOTE ABOUT DATA COLLECTION AND INTERPRETATION

During the Study, two weaknesses in the data collection process were identified—staff worksheets and submission of data on diskettes. The Study also confirmed the value of using an electronic mailing list (listserv) for communicating with participants.

Worksheet 1, Staff, was significantly revised from the one used in the 1992 ARL/RLG ILL Cost Study. The revised worksheet asked participants to list each staff member, indicate the percentage of time spent in ILL, and, of that, the percentage of time spent on borrowing and lending. While there were fewer problems than with the earlier study, the staff worksheet would benefit from additional modification in two areas. First, the column regarding percentage of time spent in ILL should be eliminated because a sufficiently large number of participants completed that line incorrectly. Participants should calculate the portion of salary devoted to ILL and report that salary, rather than reporting the full salary and percentage of time spent in ILL. Second, the method of reporting number of student assistants should be reviewed. It is unrealistic to expect participants to report individual student assistants given the number employed during the year. A separate section should be devised to report total student expenditures and the percentages devoted to borrowing and lending.

Study participants were offered a choice of submitting data on paper forms or on diskette. Most chose to submit data on paper forms. Of those who submitted data on diskette, most returned completed forms and worksheets without reformatting. However, problems arose when a few participants submitted complete worksheets, but reformatted. Because the reformatting caused a change in the structure of the worksheet, the cadre of data input staff at the University at Albany were forced to re-key entire worksheets. This additional step increased staff costs for data input and required the data entry to be reviewed by a supervisor to ensure that no keying errors were made. Accepting data on diskette eliminates the time and expense of data input, and thus, should be encouraged. However, when others use these instruments, ARL encourages them to require participants to not alter diskette versions of worksheets and questionnaires and reject them if they have been altered.

An electronic mailing list (listserv) was established for all participants and proved useful in sharing questions about interpretations of instructions or instruments. Although the questionnaire and worksheets were meant to be clear, a few questions were interpreted differently than intended. The listserv proved an effective tool for clarifying those questions and responses; ARL strongly recommends it for future studies of this scale. This communication method helped minimize variation in interpretation, and thus the variation in data.

APPENDIX M: RELATED SOURCES: A SELECTED BIBLIOGRAPHY

This section includes complete citations to publications referenced in the report as well as a list of selected readings on performance measures studies related to interlibrary loan and document delivery. Although this project was not designed to produce a systematic review of related studies, the findings of several studies and reports may be used to compare with the findings of this Study.

ARL Statistics 1995-96. Washington, DC: Association of Research Libraries, 1997.

> An annual publication that describes collections, staffing, expenditures, and service activities for the 120 members of the Association of Research Libraries. Includes a supply and demand chart that tracks annual growth of borrowing and lending from 1986-1996.

Association of Research Libraries Office of Management Services. *The CLR Benchmarking Project: Interlibrary Loan Pilot Benchmark Study.* Washington, DC: International Systems Services Corp., 1994.

> A collaborative project of ARL, the Council on Library Resources, and International Systems Services Corp. to test the applicability of benchmarking technology to research libraries. The study found that turnaround time functions as the primary measure of ILL performance.

Bjarno, Helle. "Cost Finding and Performance Measures in ILL Management." *Interlending and Document Supply* 22 (1994): 8-11.

> Based on a paper presented at the 3rd International Conference on Interlending and Document Supply held in Budapest in 1993, the paper describes a technique to measure the cost and performance of ILL services in Danish academic libraries. The paper defines in general terms performance measures for several performance indicators and provides a useful tool for looking at other studies' findings. Performance indicators are created by comparing quantitative data elements in different combinations. The purpose of the indicators is to analyze data in order to measure how well the service is performing.

Boyd, Norman. "Towards Access Services: Supply Times, Quality Control and Performance-Related Services." *Interlending & Document Supply* 25 (1997): 118-123.

> A report of a survey of six U.K. public library authorities in LASER, measuring turnaround time. Average turnaround time ranged from 17.72 to 38.6 days.

British Library Document Supply Centre. *Modelling the Economics of Interlibrary Lending.* Boston Spa: British Library Document Supply Centre, 1989.

> A report of a Coopers & Lybrand study commissioned by the British Library Document Supply Centre to provide a means of evaluating the costs of libraries' interlending activities. The report is intended to describe the computer model to collect data and the tasks used to calculate costs. The report summarizes components of projected national ILL costs in the U.K., but because of the dated nature of the study and the different interlending environment, the findings cannot be compared with the findings of the ARL ILL/DD Performance Measures Study. However, one of the valuable discussions is of how the computer model can be used to measure the effect of changing ILL procedures.

Chang, Amy. "Cost Analysis for Interlibrary Loan: A Differentiated Service." In *Managing Resource Sharing in the Electronic Age.* Amy Chang and Mary E. Jackson, eds. 112-115. New York: AMS Press, 1996.

> One example of how individual libraries used the ARL/RLG ILL Cost Study methodology. Chang argues that the ARL/RLG ILL Cost Study was one way to compute operational expenses, and suggests that a time/motion study is a second approach. However, she doesn't develop a specific methodology of how to undertake such a study.

Cost-Effectiveness of Ariel for Interlibrary Loan Copy Requests. Research Libraries Group. Available: http://www.rlg.org/arifax.html. 6 March 1996.

> A summary of a March 1996 report to RLG SHARES participants. The study demonstrates that on a cost basis alone, the use of Ariel is more cost-effective than either fax or mail for the delivery of materials.

Dickson, Stephen P., and Virginia Boucher. "A Methodology for Determining Costs of Interlibrary Lending." *Research Access Through New Technology,* edited by Mary E. Jackson. 137 - 159. New York: AMS Press, Inc., 1989.

> A methodology for estimating the cost of interlibrary lending used as the basis for the ARL/RLG ILL Cost Study. The article develops the methodology but does not test it.

Guyonneau, Christine H. "Performance Measurements for ILL: An Evaluation." *Journal of Interlibrary Loan & Information Supply* 3 (1993): 101-126.

An examination of unfilled lending requests received by the University of Indianapolis Library. Guyonneau categorizes several internal and external reasons for unavailability.

Hébert, François. *The Quality of Interlibrary Borrowing Services in Large Urban Public Libraries in Canada.* Ph.D. diss., University of Toronto, 1993.

An investigation of the quality of borrowing services in Canadian public libraries through the use of fill rate, turnaround time, and user satisfaction. Reports a fill rate of 52% and a median turnaround time of 38 days, of which 23 days represented the time it took the borrowing library to send the request to the first lender. Uses SERVQUAL to measure user expectations of ILL service quality. Reliability, ranked highest by users, scored lowest in performance. Library measures of turnaround time and fill rate did not match users' measure of service quality.

Hodgson, James G. *A Progress Report on a Study of Interlibrary Loan Costs.* Fort Collins, CO: Colorado A & M College Library, 1951.

One of the earliest ILL cost studies. Collects direct costs incurred by 32 academic libraries, two bibliographical centers, and one union catalog. Includes preliminary conclusions that there is little correlation between the average costs to individual libraries of borrowing and lending. Cost categories includes labor, materials, and transportation. Notes turnaround time of 15.6 days for requests processed by bibliographic centers and 16.4 days for requests sent directly to the lending library.

International Organization for Standardization. *Information and Documentation—Library Performance Indicators.* ISO 11620. Geneva: International Organization for Standardization, 1998.

A standard for library performance indicators developed by the International Organization for Standardization (ISO) approved in March 1998. The document includes one performance indicator relevant to the ILL/DD process, speed of interlibrary lending. This indicator is the same as turnaround time used in the ARL ILL/DD Performance Measures Study as it defines six dates with which to measure turnaround time.

Jones, Roger G. *Interlibrary Lending Costs Study 1997.* Canberra: Australian Council of Libraries and Information Services, 1997.

An update of a 1989 study of the estimated lending unit costs prepared for the Australian Council of Libraries and Information Services (ACLIS). The study includes national, state/territory, university, public, medical, and other types of libraries.

Kingma, Bruce. *The Economics of Access versus Ownership: The Costs and Benefits of Access to Scholarly Articles via Interlibrary Loan and Journal Subscriptions.* Binghamton, NY: Haworth Press, 1996.

A study of 1994 costs of access to scholarly articles for the four SUNY University Center libraries. Kingma, consulting economist to the ILL/DD Performance Measures Study, compares the cost of ownership with cost of access for articles from journals in mathematics and sciences. He quantifies the time a patron spends waiting for an article (12.95 days) and the opportunity cost for patrons waiting for material ($2.55). He develops a set of decision rules, based on level of use and subscription price, for library managers to use to choose access or ownership.

Line, Maurice B. *Measuring the Performance of Document Supply Systems* PGI-87/WS/21. Paris: General Information Programme and UNISIST, UNESCO, 1987.

A report prepared by the IFLA International Office for Universal Availability of Publications. The report defines fill rate, speed, user satisfaction, and other factors, and suggests two levels of measures: basic and desirable. Clear definitions, several data collection forms, and an emphasis on the importance of standardization make this general overview still relevant.

Lor, Peter. "Measuring the Outcomes of Southern African Interlending Requests: A Comparison of Measurement Approaches." *South African Journal of Librarianship and Information Science* 57 (1989): 362-371.

Lor examines the different ways in which fill rates can be calculated in an ILL request and clearly articulates the difference between borrowing and lending fill rates.

Naylor, Ted. "The Cost of Interlibrary Loan in a Medium-Sized College Library." *Journal of Interlibrary Loan, Document Delivery & Information Supply* 8 (1997): 51-61.

Describes the use of the ARL/RLG ILL Cost Study instrument at the Wichita State University Library. Although Naylor collected data for July 1995 to June 1996, his findings may not be directly comparable to the findings of the ARL ILL/DD Performance Measures Study because borrowing fees paid were not included in the calculation of the borrowing unit cost. The proportion of staff costs (75% for borrowing and 62% for lending) are almost opposite to figures recorded by the college libraries in this Study—62% for borrowing and 71% for lending. However, the article is a good example of how individual libraries can use a methodology developed for use by multiple libraries.

Nitecki, Danuta. *An Assessment of the Applicability of SERVQUAL Dimensions as Customer-based Criteria for Evaluating Quality of Services in an Academic Library.* Ph.D. diss., University of Maryland, 1995.

> The SERVQUAL measures were applied to three academic library services: interlibrary loan, reference, and reserves at the University of Maryland Libraries. Nitecki concludes that SERVQUAL is a reliable and valid instrument for use by academic libraries. Reliability was found to be the most important dimension to service quality for users of interlibrary loan services, confirming François Hébert's findings.

Palmour, Vernon, Edward C. Bryant, Nancy W. Caldwell, and Lucy M. Gray, comps. *A Study of the Characteristics, Costs, and Magnitude of Interlibrary Loans in Academic Libraries.* Westport, CT: Greenwood Publishing Co., 1972.

> A report prepared for the Association of Research Libraries by Westat Research, Inc. Reports the costs, characteristics of materials borrowed and loaned, and the present and future magnitude of ILL for academic libraries.

Parry, David. *Why Requests Fail: Interlibrary Lending and Document Supply Request Failures in the UK and Ireland.* British Library Research & Innovation Centre Project Report No. 59. Newcastle upon Tyne, England: Information North, 1997.

> A report of the results of a study of 54 public, university, and special libraries in the U.K. and Ireland conducted by David Parry for the Circle of Officers of National and Regional Library Systems (CONARLS). The report describes interlibrary loan failures and makes recommendations on possible solutions to the problem of failed requests.

Poll, Rosawitha, and Peter te Boekhorst. *Measuring Quality: International Guidelines for Performance Measurement in College Libraries.* IFLA Publications 76. München, Germany: K.G. Saur, 1996.

> A report written by Roswitha Poll and Peter te Boekhorst in collaboration with members of the International Federation of Library Associations' Section of University and Other General Research Libraries. The guidelines include one section relevant to interlibrary loan: interlibrary loan speed. The report suggests that the primary indicator for interlibrary loan is success rate (fill rate), defined as the proportion of documents supplied within a certain period of time. The report provides a useful log sheet and sample calculation form.

Robertson, Margaret. *Document Delivery Performance.* 2nd ed. CAUL Performance Indicator B. Canberra: Council of Australian University Librarians, 1997.

> An update of a 1995 computer program prepared by the Council of Australian University Librarians (CAUL) to collect fill rate and turnaround time data for ILL borrowing and lending. The second edition, published in fall 1997, includes an Excel spreadsheet and a user guide to the program.

Roche, Marilyn M. *The ARL/RLG Interlibrary Loan Cost Study.* Washington, DC: Association of Research Libraries, 1993.

> A joint project of the Association of Research Libraries and the Research Libraries Group. Reports costs of ILL departments in 76 North American research libraries. Finds a mean borrowing cost of $18.62, and a mean lending unit cost of $10.95, for a total of $29.55 between two research libraries. The cost methodology was used as basis for the ARL ILL/DD Performance Measures Study.

Spencer, Carol. "Random Time Sampling with Self-Observation for Library Cost Studies: Unit Costs of Interlibrary Loans and Photocopies at a Regional Medical Library." *Journal of the American Society for Information Science* 22 (May 1971): 153-160.

> A dated, but still informative, article, Spencer describes the use of random time sampling with self-observation to determine labor costs for lending in a regional medical library. The 1971 study quantifies various tasks per hour staff are able to complete and gives a detailed list of cost items and task groups.

Standing Conference of National and University Libraries. *MA/HEM: Methodology for Access/Holdings Economic Modelling.* London: Standing Conference of National and University Libraries, 1996.

> A report of a methodology developed by a consortium of Library Managers funded by the U.K. Electronic Libraries Programme. The computer program presents a spreadsheet to compare costs of obtaining documents from different sources and investigates the effects of changes in the way the costs are calculated. Wait time is used as the measure of the cost to the user of having to wait for a document. It may be a useful tool to compare the effectiveness of various lending operations and document suppliers.

State Library of South Africa. *Report on the 1996 Interlending Cost Survey and Proposed Tariff Adjustment.* Unpublished report prepared by Céléste Botha, August 1996.

Report of an annual survey of nearly 30 South African libraries prepared by the State Library of South Africa to review and set lending charges. The 1997 unpublished study reports average cost per loan, per copy, and per unfilled request. The methodology used to calculate unit cost includes staff, postage, photocopying, and delivery, and reports unit costs using a weighted average. The study is useful in how it calculates the cost of an unfilled request. The study reports a lending fill rate of 74%, somewhat less than the 85% lending fill rate reported in the ARL ILL/DD Performance Measures Study.

Taylor, Colin R. *Interlibrary Loans in Australia: Traffic Patterns and Charges, May 1989.* Canberra: National Library of Australia, 1989.

A report of a project funded by the Australian Council of Libraries and Information Services. Finds a 94% fill rate for ILL transactions in Australia. Studies filled and unfilled requests from libraries in all sectors except school libraries. Examines communication methods and charging, and includes recommendations to improve performance.

Waldhart, Thomas. "Performance Evaluation of Interlibrary Loan in the United States; A Review of Research." *Library and Information Science Research* 7 (1985): 313-331.

A comprehensive literature review of the research on the performance of interlibrary loan operations in the United States. Includes success rate, turnaround time, cost, user satisfaction, and user inconvenience for interlibrary loan. Examines document delivery communication, and calls for comprehensive and timely data to gain an understanding of the ILL system in the U.S.

Weaver-Meyers, Pat, et. al. *Journal of Library Administration* 23 (1996).

A special issue exploring strategies for redesigning ILL/DD services. Edited by Pat Weaver-Meyers, Wilbur Stolt, and Yem Fong, the ten articles examine performance of ILL from a variety of perspectives, including user satisfaction, and turnaround time.

Weaver-Meyers, Pat, Shelly Clement, and Carolyn Mahin. *Interlibrary Loan in Academic and Research Libraries: Workload and Staffing.* OP 15. Washington, DC: Association of Research Libraries, 1989.

Reports the results of a 1988 survey of ARL members and discusses the effects of workload on fill rates. Reports a mean borrowing fill rate of 83% and a mean lending fill rate of 60%, and develops a formula to calculate total requests processed per FTE.

Willemse, John. "Improving Interlending through Goal Setting and Performance Measurement." *Interlending and Document Supply* 21 (1993): 13-17.

A report of the performance of the interlibrary loan operation at the University of South Africa focusing on measuring, and improving, fill rate and turnaround time. The report measures fill rate and turnaround time, and suggests strategies to improve performance. The strategies are more applicable to North American ILL operations than the actual findings, which reflect a significantly different ILL environment.